remix

off the grid

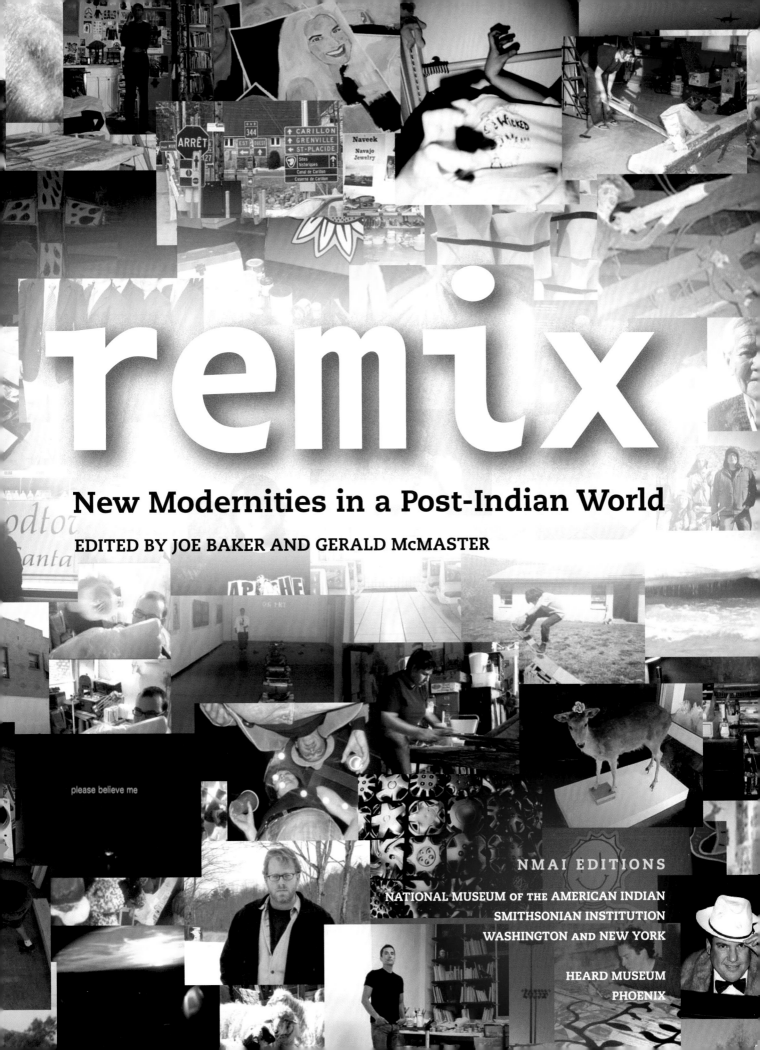

remix

New Modernities in a Post-Indian World

EDITED BY JOE BAKER AND GERALD McMASTER

please believe me

NMAI EDITIONS

NATIONAL MUSEUM OF THE AMERICAN INDIAN
SMITHSONIAN INSTITUTION
WASHINGTON AND NEW YORK

HEARD MUSEUM
PHOENIX

NMAI Head of Publications: Terence Winch
Editor: Holly Stewart
Designer: Steve Bell

First Edition

10 9 8 7 6 5 4 3 2 1

Cover:
Steven Yazzie
Sleeping with Jefferson, 2007
Hubcaps, light projections
183 x 275 x 122 cm.
Courtesy of the artist

Library of Congress Cataloging-in-Publication Data

Remix : new modernities in a post-Indian world / edited by Joe Baker and Gerald McMaster.
-- 1st ed.
    p. cm.
  "Published in conjunction with the exhibition of the same name, on view at the Heard Museum in Phoenix, Arizona, from October 6, 2007, to April 27, 2008, and at the George Gustav Heye Center, National Museum of the American Indian, in New York, New York, from May 26 through September 30, 2008."
  Includes bibliographical references.
  ISBN 978-1-933565-10-1 (alk. paper)
  1. Art, American--21st century--Exhibitions. 2. Indian art--North America--21st century--Exhibitions. 3. Indians of North America--Ethnic identity--Exhibitions. 4. Racially mixed people--North America--Psychology--Exhibitions. I. Baker, Joe, 1946- II. McMaster, Gerald, 1953- III. Heard Museum. IV. National Museum of the American Indian (U.S.). George Gustav Heye Center.
N6503.R46 2007
704.03'97073074753--dc22

  2007033761

The National Museum of the American Indian, Smithsonian Institution, is dedicated to working in collaboration with the indigenous peoples of the Americas to protect and foster Native cultures throughout the Western Hemisphere. The museum's publishing program seeks to augment awareness of Native American beliefs and lifeways, and to educate the public about the history and significance of Native cultures.

For information about the National Museum of the American Indian, visit the NMAI website at **www.AmericanIndian.si.edu**.

To support the museum by becoming a member, call 1-800-242-NMAI (6624) or visit www.AmericanIndian.si.edu and click on Membership & Giving.

The mission of the Heard Museum of Native Cultures and Art is to educate the public about the heritage and living cultures and arts of Native peoples, with an emphasis on the peoples of the Southwest.

For information about the Heard Museum and its programs, visit **www.heard.org**.

For information on membership, or other ways to support the Heard, see www.heard.org/NETCOMMUNITY/Page.aspx?&pid=184&srcid=197.

Published in conjunction with the exhibition *Remix : New Modernities in a Post-Indian World*, on view at the Heard Museum in Phoenix from October 6, 2007, to April 27, 2008, and at the George Gustav Heye Center, National Museum of the American Indian, in New York, from May 26 through September 30, 2008.

Contents

The Challenge of This Moment

Contemporary art exhibitions often challenge museum visitors, especially at institutions like the Heard Museum, where a visitor's expectations may be to see the traditional masterworks of the cultures of the Southwest. Notwithstanding people's expectations, it is important that work like that of the fifteen artists in *Remix: New Modernities in a Post-Indian World* be exposed in museums. What better place to do that than the Heard and the National Museum of the American Indian?

The challenge presented by contemporary, avant-garde art is not simply whether or not we like the work, but rather what we can learn from it. It is a challenge we hope you will embrace. Curator Joe Baker, in his essay, describes *Remix* as "an exhibition of rigor and complexity." His colleague, critic and art historian Eleanor Heartney, writes that the artists in *Remix* favor a "more promiscuous approach to art and identity." Clearly, there is a commitment by the younger generation of artists shown here to get beyond the traditional artistic obsession with Native identity and tribal customs. Their commitment is to a "post-Indian world"—without the limitations or expectations of earlier times.

There is another common point of departure for the artists in *Remix*—beyond that of personal, individual freedoms. If anything holds these fifteen artists together, it is the desire to be of the moment. As Joe Baker says: "Their discourse is about today's reality." And that reality is shaped by popular culture, politics, current events, and the changing social mores of the 21st century.

I may not need to issue another challenge, especially to the artists in this exhibition, yet I cannot resist. The challenge is to *all* artists, and it is a simple one: Search your soul, find something that is uniquely yours, and express it through your own creativity. Listen to the wisdom of the great American abstract expressionist painter Robert Motherwell:

Remix artists:
Dustinn Craig
Fausto Fernandez
Luis Gutierrez
David Hannan
Gregory Lomayesva
Brian Miller
Franco Mondini-Ruiz
Kent Monkman
Nadia Myre
Alan Natachu
Hector Ruiz
Anna Tsouhlarakis
Kade Twist
Bernard Williams
Steven Yazzie

When contemporary artists talk among themselves about other artists, first they weed out what is meaningless in terms of repetition and conventional clichés; then they reject what may show more talent, but is essentially false, without inner integrity, whatever the mode of expression. Much of what passes for art is not different from the rest of society, a series of lies, for exterior reasons, or occasionally from self-delusion, or most often from inherited prejudices and *a priori* conceptions. True originality is that which originates in one's own being. Nothing else is worth consideration or preservation in this gallery.

On behalf of the Heard Museum, I thank everyone who has given so much of themselves in making this exhibition possible. Your lifelong dedication to American Indian art, to museums, and to their educational mission is wonderfully expressed in the challenges presented in this provocative exhibition.

—FRANK H. GOODYEAR, JR.
Director, Heard Museum

Dustinn Craig
7 Mile Sk8 Krew, from
4-Wheel Warpony, 2007
Video
Courtesy of the artist

On the Edge

Welcome to the National Museum of the American Post-Indian! This new name will no doubt surprise the United States Congress, which created the museum way back in 1989, and may bemuse many of our longtime members, myself included. But it is a change the next generation of artists and curators assures me is long overdue.

Forgive my irony, which I offer entirely without malice, in the spirit of the witty and iconoclastic art confronting you throughout these pages. Joe Baker (Delaware), Lloyd Kiva New Curator of Fine Art at the Heard Museum, and Gerald McMaster (Plains Cree), curator of Canadian art at the Art Gallery of Ontario, have brought together a remarkable group of fifteen contemporary artists of Native heritage from throughout the United States, Canada, and Mexico. For this project, Baker and McMaster have appropriated a title, *Remix*, from global hip-hop culture. There, it refers to the practice of using altered, but recognizable, pieces of earlier works to create new music, a technique that takes advantage of the astonishing tools of our digital age. Here, the curators offer remixing as a metaphor for contemporary concepts of identity, reflected in these artists' painting, sculpture, photography, video, and installation art.

Identity has long been a theme of this museum's programs. Our inaugural exhibitions at the George Gustav Heye Center in New York in the early 1990s made the point that, for all their beauty and aesthetic genius, very few of the masterworks on view in our galleries were created as art in any Western sense of the word. Rather, the majority of these treasures were made as manifestations of individual and, predominantly, cultural identity—commemorations of defining events, and means of recording who a people were, what they experienced, and what they believed.

The works shown here, however, unlike most of those in the museum's unparalleled archaeological and ethnographic collections, were made quite consciously as art, and they express each artist's personal interpretation of identity no more, and no less, than contemporary art created by non-Natives. For the community of artists in our time, identity is both a more idiosyncratic and a more fluid concept, a river in which currents of gender and personal experience, along with race, nationality, and cultural heritage, mix and remix, in continual re-creation.

This, then, is the post-Indian world, though, of course, the subtitle, with its reference to new modernities, is a pun on postmodernism as well. With that play on words, Baker and McMaster are taking a dig at the past role of museums. No longer will curators acquiesce to the perpetuation of national myths, or the objectification of other peoples through the self-congratulatory collecting and exhibiting of their material culture! At the risk of sounding self-satisfied, I think that species of culturally arrogant museum is well on its way to extinction. In the last fifteen years, NMAI has received its share of criticism. Yet, the content of that critical commentary has changed over time. Recently, when writers and museum visitors have taken issue with our efforts, it is because we have fallen short of the high bar we set for ourselves, not because people believe we should do things in the old ways. We welcome such criticism, though I am also pleased to note that books and exhibitions of contemporary Native art have been among the most influential and best-received projects we have produced during my tenure.

Apropos of that, I'd like to share an exchange from a panel discussion at the Heye Center opening and book signing for another recent contemporary art exhibition—*Off the Map: Landscape in the Native Imagination*, curated by Kathleen Ash-Milby (Navajo). During a question-and-answer session, the gifted writer Paul Chaat Smith (Comanche) asked the five artists whose paintings and video were on view if they were concerned that the label "Native art" reduced their work to genre status. In fact, none of the five thought of him- or herself as a "Native artist," but neither did any of them find the designation limiting. After a few moments' pause, Emmi Whitehorse (Navajo) said that if anything about her work reflected her tribal background, it is that she has never been reluctant to depict beauty. Then the painter James Lavadour (Walla Walla), whose home and studio are on the Umatilla Indian Reservation in Oregon, added, "There is such a sense of possibility now in so many Native communities, so much optimism. This is an exciting time to be an Indian." In the answers to Smith's question lay both a crystalline insight into Navajo cultural values and a firsthand characterization of life in Indian Country quite at odds with the depictions available in the non-Native press.

So, although I understand what Baker and McMaster mean by a post-Indian world—and I am delighted to have worked together with them and the Heard Museum to present this wonderful art—I would argue that the National Museum of the American Indian will make its greatest contribution to cultural knowledge by continuing to be an institution whose identity is unambiguously Indian, though one that questions, always, what that means. Or, to paraphrase Jam Master Jay, we need to be on the edge, and to keep our eyes open.

—W. RICHARD WEST, JR.
(Southern Cheyenne and member of the Cheyenne and Arapaho Tribes of Oklahoma)
Founding Director, National Museum of the American Indian, Smithsonian Institution

Acknowledgements

We are grateful to the artists whose work is shown in *Remix*, and to the galleries and collectors who have lent pieces to the exhibition and given permission to publish the images on these pages. We owe special thanks to Joe Baker (Delaware) and Gerald McMaster (Plains Cree), for the vision and passion they bring to advocacy for living artists. We also thank critic Eleanor Heartney and John Haworth (Cherokee), director of the George Gustav Heye Center, for the scholarship and experience reflected in their essays for this book. John also worked tirelessly to promote this partnership between the National Museum of the American Indian and the Heard Museum.

Many people on the Heard staff made essential contributions to the success of this project, including curator of collections Diana Pardue, curatorial administrative assistant Angie Holmes (Hopi), artist assistant Shaliyah Ben (Navajo), and associate registrar Marcus Monenerkit. Exhibit and design manager Manuelito Wheeler (Navajo), exhibit designer Melissa Martinez, senior graphic designer Kevin Coochwytewa (Isleta/Hopi), preparator Dan Johnson, and fabricator Phil Douglas played key roles in mounting the exhibition in Phoenix. Additional thanks are owed to Gina Laczko, education services manager; Nicole Haas, marketing communications manager; Debbie Drye (Hopi/Paiute), Heard Museum receptionist; and Wendy Weston (Navajo), the museum's outstanding director of American Indian relations. The Heard Museum Guild has been steadfast in supporting Native art. We are also grateful to the Heard Museum Council for their ongoing support of contemporary exhibitions, and to the Arizona Commission on the Arts for assistance to contemporary artists.

This project would not have been possible without the generosity of the Virginia Piper Charitable Trust.

The NMAI publications staff—especially head of publications Terence Winch, managing editor Ann Kawasaki, editor Holly Stewart, designer Steve Bell, design assistant Angelia Collins (Lumbee), and researcher Leah Gibson-Blackfeather (Lakota)—produced this beautiful and lively book. Betsy Gordon managed NMAI's work on the *Remix* project with determination and patience. The project team in New York helped shape the exhibition from the earliest discussions, especially Peter Brill, Heye Center deputy assistant director for exhibitions and public programs; designers Susanna Stieff, Barbara Suhr, and Kate Johnson; education and public programs coordinator Shawn Termin (Lakota), audiovisual coordinator Patrick Glynn, project assistant Robert Mastrangelo, collections manager Dominique Cocuzza, and a crew of exhibition specialists led by Stacey Jones and John Richardson. We are also grateful to Lucia DeRespinis, director of development at the Heye Center, and Ann Marie Sekeres and Trey Moynihan, of the Office of Public Affairs, for their support.

—FRANK GOODYEAR, JR. & W. RICHARD WEST, JR.

Interventions: Making a New Space for Indigenous Art

At the center of every territory is another border; at the heart of every identity is an assemblage of other identities.

—Alan Gilbert

Over the course of working with Gerald McMaster to develop *Remix: New Modernities in a Post-Indian World*, my interpretation of the goals in presenting this group of artists and their art has expanded and coalesced into irregular shapes, personal moments of recognition, fear, elation, frustration, or joy. Given my artist's background, my understanding of the role of a curator may be somewhat different from that of my contemporaries. A curator is asked to build bridges between artists and institutions, between art and its audience. A curator is someone who brings representations together, knowing that there may well be conflicts among them. No bridge stands without tension. That said, I do not try to position myself in front of the artists' work, but to stand to the side, as a facilitator alert to the artists' voices and to their complex engagements with their imaginations and the world. I would never presume to use an artist's work to illustrate a concept or idea. I'm interested instead in constructing a new platform for indigenous artists— a resistance model for how their art is presented, discussed, and contextualized. With *Remix*, as I've listened and observed, seeking to feel the mood or temperature of this artists' collective, old stories have emerged, re-invented themselves, and become relevant once again.

The year is 1957, the place a small town named Dewey in the state of Oklahoma. I am eleven years old. Excavation has begun on North Creek Street, a block from my childhood home. That 1907 bungalow, a white clapboard structure with a sagging front porch and creaky pinewood floors, appears heavy on the landscape, weighed down by family secrets, whispered stories shared around Saturday-night pitch games with relatives, gatherings lasting sometimes until first light.

Bernard Williams
Charting America, 2002–present
Wood & cardboard cutouts
488 x 762 cm.
Courtesy of the artist and
Ethan Cohn Gallery

C. A. Comer house,
designed by Bruce Goff.
Dewey, Oklahoma

Perhaps the events unfolding then were some kind of rite of passage, an inevitable coming of age played out during the Cold War period following World War II. Or perhaps creativity was being unlocked in me, propelling me toward an attraction for the original that still moves me today. Whatever the case, mediocrity no longer held my attention. During the months ahead, my interest would be focused on North Creek Street, as cranes set into place massive beams defining the pitched triangular roof of the C. A. Comer residence, designed by the architect Bruce Goff. Tethered to the ground by cables, the structure hovered over the lawn like a spaceship. Diagonal slices of glass cut through the brick exterior creating transparent portals to interior spaces. The roof floated above the exterior walls like a low-hovering cloud. I was transfixed.

I was not the only one who noticed the strange new house on Creek Street. Cars lined up on Sunday afternoons, slowly cruising the construction site. There were incidents of vandalism, and letters to the editor of the local newspaper referring to the residence as a monstrosity, an eyesore. The Comers themselves were rumored to be communists, progressives, individuals to watch out for.

How could something so original, fresh, forward-looking, exciting be so maligned? How could contemporary architecture illicit such angry responses of disgust, outrage, suspicion?

Fast forward to 2006 and the Heard Museum in Phoenix, Arizona, where *Artspeak*, a series of solo and group exhibitions by indigenous artists, was then in its third season. The range of work included video, new media, and installation art as well as the more familiar forms of sculpture, painting and drawing, and photography. *Artspeak* exhibitions were noticed by the larger arts community, with reviews appearing in *Art in America*, *Art Papers*, and other journals, and art museums from New York to Paris expressing interest in the series. A home run! But wait: Letters to the museum director employed declarative language to say, "Shame on the Heard!" Rumors questioned the authenticity of the artists and the squandering of valuable museum resources on "claptrap." Accusations that the curators supported political propaganda were common. I took to wondering whether I might be accused of espionage.

As I thought about the larger issue behind such mean-spirited words, the reactions to *Artspeak* felt strangely familiar—like 1957. Why are indigenous artists not allowed to celebrate the present as other artists do? Why do we require of Native artists a myth or fantasy, an iconography? What became of the celebrated ideal of multiculturalism, a world composed of ever-changing blends and mixtures?

In fact, as society has moved from the industrial age to the new global economy, the desire to define the "exotic" the "other" has intensified. In *The Culture Game*, the Nigerian-born, London-educated art historian Olu Oguibe states:

For those who come to it from backgrounds outside Europe (the "ethnics," "postcolonials," "minorities," all those who have ancestry, connections, or affiliations "elsewhere"), the arena of mainstream cultural practice in the West, at least in the visual arts, is a doubly predictable space— first, because it is a game space and you have to know the rules of the game, and second, because [as in] any other game, such aspirants have little chance of success because it is predetermined they should fail. Though they may know the rules—and most who have the patience to understudy it do, bitterly so—the game is nevertheless inherently stacked against them because their presence, and worse still their success, causes a fault through an outwardly solid wall of history that ought to bar them as serious contenders. Of course, the understanding is that they belong in a different space, should create work of a particular flavor, deal with a certain set of themes, exhibit in particular avenues in particular locations outside the mainstream, or be prepared to offer work of a particular nature to earn momentary mainstream acknowledgment, after which they are quietly returned to obscurity. [1]

Most indigenous artists understand this treacherous reality: The presentation of contemporary non-European art cannot be separated from historical convention, from the "genuinely European tradition of the 'collecting of cultures' that involves scientific, artistic, and institutional practices. Examples include: curiosity cabinets, museums, universities, world's fairs, encyclopedias, orientalism, exoticism, travel writing, cartography, adventure novels, ethnography, and documentary films."[2] This 500-year legacy of theory and custom still informs museum work. What is "open storage," much favored today as a mechanism for making permanent collections accessible to viewers, but the refashioning of curiosity cabinets? Or "first-person voice," other than another lens of interpretation carefully chosen by an organizing institution? Art books and exhibitions featuring the first-person voice are as likely as any other sort to be composed of vast arrays of disparate objects detached from their social and community histories, brought together to be gazed upon and perhaps admired by the dominant culture; just as likely to be highly controlled presentations focusing on religious practice, ritual, trade and exchange, social and domestic interaction, and a mythical timelessness reinforcing the primal and natural, clichéd and thoroughly scripted. This colonial yoke of cultural interpretation forces artists into the position of "cultural representatives." This, as described by Oguibe, is the current "call for identity."

This legacy is particularly burdensome for contemporary indigenous artists who seek to explore, through their artistic skill and intellectual courage, a rich and diverse reservoir of past and present inspirations. Can the artist truly be free to pursue the dictates of his or her own desires and resist "the exoticist demands of the West?" *Remix* seeks to examine current ideas surrounding this question. In their work, fifteen artists from across the Western Hemisphere explore the very edges of our human experience. Collectively, these artists probe the global movement of ideas, search for a new language of artistic practice, and push the boundaries of the expected. Heirs to rich traditions, they define their moment by dismantling and rebuilding, like DJs borrowing and building new sounds, beats, actions, engagements. Many of the artists whose works are represented here examine the terrain of their worlds while paying careful attention to how their lives play out in the broader American experience. Perhaps they relate to Fab Five Freddy's fabulous summation of postmodernism and the hip-hop aesthetic: to "take a bit from here and a bit from there and bring them all together . . . yet not forgetting history."[3]

Bernard Williams's *Charting America* provides a clear and direct example. Art historian and critic Kathryn Kramer observes, "These cultural charts evoke a nonlinear historical consciousness at odds with the notion of a progressive evolution from past through present to future that marks the historical consciousness of Western nations."[4] Black cutouts resembling silhouettes—art for the common people in colonial New England—arranged in horizontal bands against a white background provide cultural clues to Western expansion and the societies that have inhabited North America. The cutouts move across the visual field like streaming text messages in Times Square, creating a new language of postcolonial cultural mixtures. Williams has researched the myth of the American West, combing archives, museums, and historical societies throughout the United States. His studio, on Chicago's westside, is itself a vast archive of references, books, and publications. *Charting America*, embedded with narrative symbols of a collision of American Indians, Hispanics, Africans, and Europeans, rewrites American history. The viewer is reminded of a story unfolding, with all the tropes of colonial exclusivity giving way to a more complex tale of past and present.

Enter, center stage, Sylvia Gallagher, during one of those white-hot moments of transition as I struggle to re-invent my art, myself, after the Vietnam War. She at fifty has abandoned Francis I sterling and ormolu candelabras for meditation, The Joy of Sex, *jade, and vodka, blue work shirts, the ceramic art of Karen Karns, M. C. Richards, Paul Soldner, and Paulus Berensohn, and "dancing" clay bowls she fires in a backyard kiln. Sylvia introduces me to balsamic vinaigrette and simple green salads—instructing me how to properly prepare and slice green onions on the diagonal. To crayfish and boiled shrimp, chicory-flavored coffee, and scotch before noon. To the Louisiana custom of lagniappe, the little extra thing a storekeeper adds to a customer's purchase—the unexpected gift, which made its way to Creole, via Spanish, from the Quechua word* yapay, *"to give more."*

Sylvia rescued me from a tree one day when I drunkenly admitted that I no longer knew who I was, and drove me in a Datsun station wagon on a highway south, gathering red wildflowers along the way. At Caddo Lake she stopped, inquiring after a man named Lomax at shadowy fish shacks along the sloughs of dark red waters. In good time she passed me on to Lomax and his canoe, with the promise to return at eight that night. Lomax hoisted onboard a cooler of Miller Lite, a guitar, a bag of sandwiches, and said, "Get in." Low to the water, we silently moved in a yellowish light among narrow passages of giant cypress. "You can call me Dave," he finally spoke. "What name do you go by?"

Bernard Williams
Charting America, 2002–present
Wood & cardboard cutouts
488 x 762 cm.
Courtesy of the artist and
Ethan Cohn Gallery

"I used to sell insurance in Dallas, but came back here to the lake where I grew up. I know these waters inside and out, I can take you into places you'll never find on a map. . . . Wanna beer?" "I met my first wife when I was stationed in San Diego in the Navy, that didn't last long, she went out with her girlfriends one night and never came back." "Are you married?" "I've been work'n on a new song, how about if I sing it for you?" "Are you an artist?" "I've gotta take a piss." The canoe rocking side to side he let go a yellow arc into the lake. "I've always said, you shake it more than twice you're playing with it."

Lomax never stopped talking once he started. Blue heron watched, and the lotus fields opened up yielding to the canoe while I occupied myself with thoughts about the Caddo people. The canoe slid up and onto the soft mud bank just ahead of eight p.m. There above the rise I could see Sylvia's headlights waiting. "You take care of yourself, let me know when you get back down this way again." "You tell 'em back home that Lomax took you to places nobody's ever seen." Sylvia and I drove on the back roads toward Shreveport as I continued to think about the Caddo people in Anadarko, all they once had, all that was lost.

Nadia Myre
Portrait in Motion, 2002
Video
Courtesy of Galerie Art Mûr
© Nadia Myre/licensed by
SODART, Montréal, and
VAGA, New York

Nadia Myre's *Portrait in Motion* presents the artist in a sculpture—a canoe—constructed one half of birch bark, the other half, aluminum. In this four-minute video, the artist is paddling toward the viewer. Bird sounds and breaking water can be heard. The viewer is forced to make certain decisions regarding the work's interpretation. Some audiences might find a perverse fulfillment in watching the Native seemingly at one with the natural environment. Critic James Martin understands the artist's actions as "subtly riffing on the well-worn film image of 'spotting an Indian amidst the beauty of the wilderness.'"[5] First Nations artist Robert Houle suggests that the video:

> celebrates Myre's original culture and provides a vehicle for addressing a repressed history and culture that lurks beneath the tourism industry's representations of the Canadian wilderness as uninhabited. . . . It serves notice that the social and economic development of our nation state began with the adoption of the birch bark canoe by fur traders, *coureurs de bois*, *voyageurs*, and white settlers. Constructing a life-sized canoe of two distinct halves (birch bark and aluminum) makes us beautifully visible. Her object becomes more than cottage country, recreational equipment; it becomes something representing our contribution to society.[6]

Playing on the voyeuristic tendency of how Native people are perceived by the art establishment, Kent Monkman's installation *Shooting Geronimo* doesn't hold back. The painted tipi, perhaps a stand-in for an adult video booth, features sexually charged cowboys and Indians acting out in a highly eroticized scene, complete with a Monument Valley backdrop. The cast, including Thosh Collins, Quetzal Guerrero, and Alex Meraz, masterfully fulfills the dominant culture's every fleshly desire of the exotic "other." Caramel to cinnamon and buff, they subvert and dislodge society's appetite for the sensationalized Native. By repositioning video in a three-dimensional space, Monkman has freed the medium from the conventional screen, or monitor, claiming a place on the gallery floor. According to Liz Kotz, such actions "offer rich possibilities for rethinking and restructuring these core relationships—between viewing subject, moving or still image, architectural space, and time—that are so fundamental to modern visual culture."[7] We expect nothing less from Monkman. His earlier series of paintings, *The Moral Landscape*—appropriations of the romantic landscapes by 19th-century American painters Albert Bierstadt, Thomas Cole, George Catlin, and Paul Kane—have challenged Christian ideologies and the notion of Manifest Destiny. According to Monkman, the paintings:

> investigate the relationship of sexuality to conquest, xenophobia, and imperialism. In my versions, the familiar players in North American history (Indians, explorers, and cowboys) are reconfigured in provocative and humorous sexual vignettes set against sublime landscapes. Emulating the context of the original paintings as ethnological documentation, or pictures from a travelogue, my paintings play with power dynamics within sexuality to challenge historical assumptions of sovereignty, art, commerce, and colonialism.[8]

It is Ash Wednesday, and seeing the marks on practicing Catholics has placed me on the edge of some childhood memory, a memory that doesn't present itself until near dusk. Late that day, I call Maxine, my 89-year-old cousin. "Do you remember anything about ash marks on the face from back home?"

"Yes," she replied in that slow and deliberate way when you know the memory is there if you give it time. "Betty and I when we were kids would go and stay with Grandmother Katie Whiteturkey, northwest of Bartlesville. If we were to go out at night—like a Stomp Dance or something—she'd take a little ash and mark our faces. Your mother probably did the same for you. That's to protect you from a manitu, the blood spirits. Or, if we were playing out back near the woods toward evening, Katie would always call us in. When I'd ask her why we couldn't stay out and play, she'd tell us about the 'rolling black ball' [blood spirits] that come out at night and roll through the woods. If you're out there it could strike you at the knees and you'd go lame, or it might take you to a place and you'd be disorientated and couldn't find your way home. That's what you're remembering, the blood spirits, from back home."

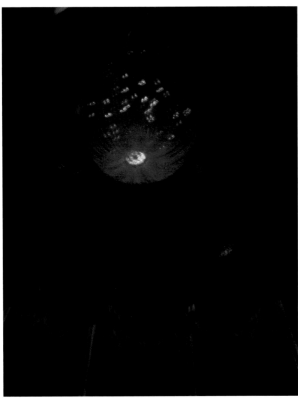

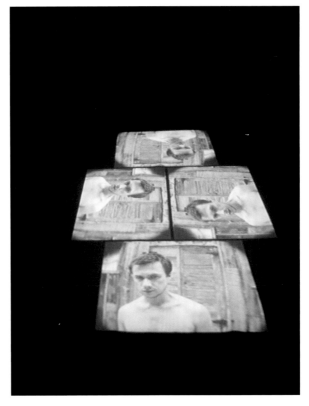

ABOVE:
Anna Tsouhlarakis
Let's Dance!, 2004
Video
Courtesy of the artist

LEFT:
Brian Miller
Dodge, 2003
Inkjet print
71 x 112 cm.
Courtesy of the artist

Sarah, 2003
Inkjet print
71 x 112 cm.
Courtesy of the artist

Photography has a problematic history for indigenous people. In the hands of ethnographers, photography has often been used to make voyeuristic incursions into traditional rituals and practices. The travel and tourism industry, too, has placed at our disposal likenesses of powwows, hoop contests, ever-colorful parades of "dancing Indians" in resplendent attire. As journalistic or ethnographic instrument, the camera has helped perpetuate certain stereotypes of culture.

Occasionally, however—more and more often, recently—indigenous artists have claimed ownership of photography as an artistic medium of engagement. In a photographic series chronicling the events along an empty road in New Hampshire in the fall of 2001, Brian Miller tells a haunting tale entitled *Black North*. Far from being symbols or icons of the "other," Miller's exquisite black-and-white windows to stories may well have more in common with Hank Williams's "Lost Highway," or AC/DC's "Highway to Hell." According to Miller, "Looking over the negatives and some proofs I saw a record of a trip, a descent into a psychologically dark place. The experience made me into something else. Certain images began to remind me of Dante's *Inferno*, his own descent into hell. I began to see the old dirt roads and abandoned places of New Hampshire as a modern analogue for hell. My old Ford pickup and Sarah Ophelia were my guides."[9]

Anna Tsouhlarakis's video *Let's Dance!* was created during a residency at the Skowhegan School of Painting and Sculpture in Maine, where, over the course of thirty days, she danced thirty dances with people from diverse cultures. The multiplicity of traditional dances, including the hora, Indian two-step, Harlem shake, and Irish jig, allows the artist entry into "other" space, while placing the "other" into the artist's space. Through this out-of-joint participation, Tsouhlarakis constructs a kind of pictorial grammar, creating a certain time-out from cultural identity. She creates a radically neutral time.

Two Chevrolet Bel Airs are parked two spaces apart on Main Street. My mother's two sisters are distanced by a forty-year silence taken since to death. As different as alike, they hold tight some long-ago family secret.

Aunt Pearl had certain "Methodist ways." She wore only brown and married but one time, her hair pulled back in a tightly held bun. She was forever shading her eyes with her hand. She was polite, but cool. Her white husband was a veteran of World War II and worked the lease on her allotment lands; together they had one son. They lived in a small, unpainted lease house on the eastern edge of the allotment. Her lands wrapped around Mother's to the north and west. Her wells were pumping; ours were not. One late afternoon we drove out to the land, something Mother liked to do. It was tornado season.

Soon, a greenish-yellow cloud fell over us as the winds kicked up the trees along the river. Mother looked to the east and said, "Get into the car, now!" My sister and I clamored into the back seat, watching the sky through the back windshield as the car lurched and churned through earthen ruts toward the gravel section line. No words were spoken as Mother gripped the steering wheel and turned the car into the driveway at Pearl's place, under the tall locust trees. My sister and I saw the cellar doors just north of the garage. "Wait here," Mother directed as she got out of the car and moved purposefully toward the back door. Pearl stepped into the yard, shielding her eyes with her hand, looking toward the car and up at the sky. Suddenly, Mother turned and bolted toward the car. In one quick motion we were in reverse heading fast toward town. The dust behind shielding the sky. No words spoken.

Aunt Betty wore only color, had one son, and married five times. She wore Chanel perfume and couture fashions purchased in Kansas City. Her beauty was unchallenged, seductive, and misleading. She fought furiously for love, stabbing those who deceived her with the broken ends of beer bottles. Her white husband was a veteran of World War II and worked at various jobs. Her allotment lands were gone. She never spoke of Pearl.

We walked on Main Street, our silence shaped by unspoken actions long ago. Refugees of U.S. policy, the Allotment Act, pious Christian thought, greed. Our lives were lived always spaces apart, in worlds split by silence. We walked.

Paulo Herkenhoff, in his essay "Brazil: The Paradoxes of an Alternative Baroque," speaks to the "historical forging of bodies during the making of the Americas—by violence, by sexual encounters, by gender politics, by the anatomy lessons of science, by religion, and by art."[10] Franco Mondini-Ruiz brings this reference to mind. Born in San Antonio, Texas, to an Italian father and a Mexican mother, Mondini-Ruiz's life and art play out as an endless range of marvelous choices. Abandoning a career in law to commit his energies to full-time art-making, Mondini-Ruiz is an example of a passionate artist pushing both buttons and boundaries, mixing tastes and cultures in a contemporary moment of performance. He pushes the envelope of art as commodity, combining a quixotic idealism—making art accessible to all people—with a keen business acumen, the modernist legacy of Donald Judd with the over-the-top visual excess of borderlands *lingua franca*.

I first met Mondini-Ruiz in the summer of 2006 at the Liberty Bar, a crooked structure put up in 1890 as the Liberty Schooner Saloon, on the corner of Josephine and Avenue A, near downtown San Antonio. Notorious for its bitter greens

Franco Mondini-Ruiz
Rosa Mexicana,
from *Counterpoint*, 2007
Acrylic on canvas
25 x 20 cm.
Courtesy of the artist and
Frederieke Taylor Gallery

Cowboys Out of Indians,
from *Counterpoint*, 2007
Acrylic on canvas
20 x 25 cm.
Courtesy of the artist and
Frederieke Taylor Gallery

and diverse clientele, the Liberty served as the starting gate for a whirlwind encounter with Mondini-Ruiz's "social sculpture." Just returned from a six-year living experience in Manhattan, he was rediscovering his hometown. We visited artists' studios, mainstream museums and galleries, the last tiny section of the San Antonio River in its natural state before being diverted to underground concrete channels, and his grandmother's house on the westside, now converted into his studio and living space. Would his coming home to San Antonio signal a return to the *Infinito Botanica*—a process work from the 1990s, the work that launched his career? As Elizabeth Armstrong and Victor Zamudio-Taylor explain:

> In the mid 1990s, Mondini-Ruiz purchased a *botanica* on South Flores, in an old Mexican-American barrio . . . that catered to adherents of folk-healing practices such as *curanderismo* and *santeria*. Renaming the storefront "Infinito Botanica and Gift Shop," he continued to offer objects and advice that blend different spiritual trends with Catholic religiosity. At the same time he transformed the space into a boutique, art gallery, and salon. Alongside an array of products used for spiritual cleansing and folk medicine—incense, talismans, special soaps and waters, images of *santos* and *virgenes*, herbs, oils, devotional candles, *milagros*, and fetishes—he offered a cornucopia of objects for sale, ranging from folk and hobo art, to readymades and art from Texan and Mexican artists.[11]

Phoenix artist Hector Ruiz grew up in border towns in Texas, crossing to the Mexican town of Piedras Negras to visit family. Ruiz brings an intense activism to the woodcarvings and linoprints he creates, using *hecho a mano*—the hand-made—to expose the "blind materialism, overconsumption, and self-interest of the American way." Shunning mechanization to create his provocative wood sculptures, the artist carves away the façade of rhetoric and language and cuts to the core of inequity and divisiveness in the human race. Revealing hidden histories in which racist acts today are linked to those of the past, Ruiz underscores the reality of racial oppression as a clash between Western thought (power/superiority) and indigenous culture. For Ruiz, identity is symbolically played out on the streets, in the museums and cultural institutions, and in the bedrooms of Phoenix every day. Art critic Lara Taubman notes, "Ruiz's work encompasses the broad, complex, and often painful world particular to the Arizona and neighboring Mexican landscape. United States and Mexican border issues, immigration, conflicts of gender and sexuality, and urban development oblivious to the needs of the individual and the landscape create a combinative world that is seen through Ruiz's own emotionally critical lens instead of through a universal one."[12]

Fausto Fernandez's collaged and painted surfaces seem to turn inward to a self-reflective space, exploring the complexities of intimate relationships. Like blueprints, sewing patterns, maps, his works appear as guides to complex journeys

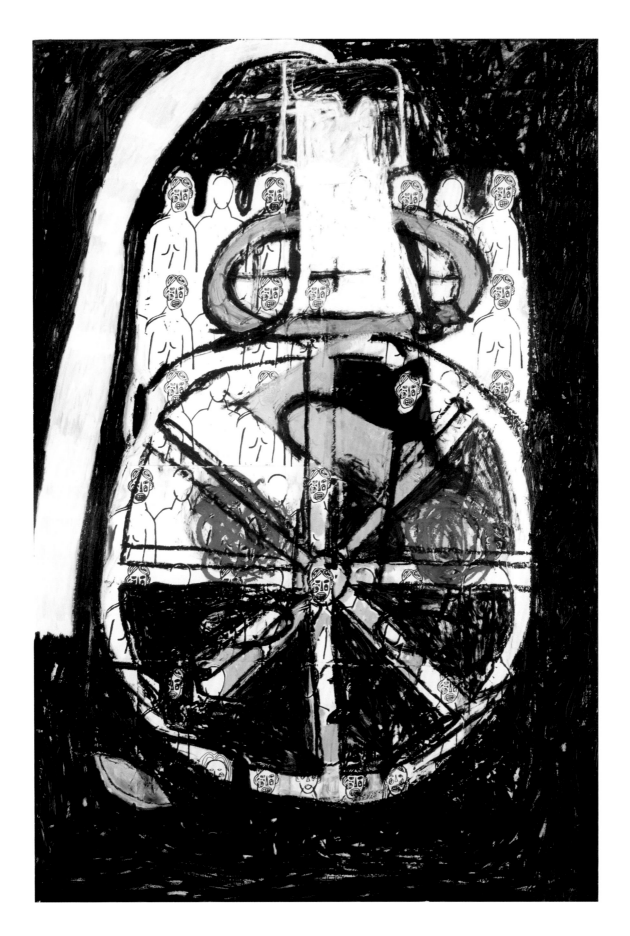

Luis Gutierrez
Voodoo Lives for Your Pins, 2005
Mixed media
132 x 137 cm.
Courtesy of the artist

or skills. One begins to understand that, for this artist, life is a board game. What is not clearly stated here is that the rules of the game are set, and not always fair.

For Luis Gutierrez, art is a companion, a fact he realized while studying at Richmond University in London, when he began to miss brown-skinned people, Chicano culture, the familiar. Later in life, when Gutierrez was diagnosed with multiple sclerosis, art became for him a language to process issues around health and well-being. Loaded with references to popular culture, his imagery details a very personal and highly charged reality, the urban Chicano experience close to home and cut down to the bone.

The loud song of the locust drones in the mid-afternoon heat. A pickup pulls alongside the curb out front, my uncle shouting, "Come on, take a ride with me out to the lease. I'll have you back here before your mother gets off work." Happy for any diversion, I climb onto the seat of the truck. It smells of sweat, oil, and cigarettes; a crumpled pack of Viceroys rolls back and forth along the floorboard.

"Your dad gone again?" My uncle knew our life well. Another binge that would probably last for several days, then a few days of quiet before the loud arguments would start in the kitchen and play out throughout the house, sometimes spilling into the night as Mother frantically loaded us into the car and we drove to my aunt's house.

Climbing out of the truck at the familiar pump house, a mile north and west of Dewey, my uncle turned and said, "This won't take but a minute, then we'll head on up to the river on the four mile road." I knew exactly our destination. The fork of the Little Caney is the site of the first camps after we were moved from the Kansas Reserve one hundred years before. The Delaware cemetery is near. I felt strange about going there. I waited as he checked gauges, fixing his attention on the whirling machinery. Dust particles floating trancelike in the heat inside the cab of the truck occupied my interest.

"All done," as he climbed into the truck setting a course toward the river. Turning onto a narrow dirt road winding closer to the trees along the river, I could smell the damp sweet breath of the slow-moving green water. Giant cottonwoods clattered above. "Come on, we're going for a swim," my uncle reaching behind the seat of the truck for a towel. I froze at that moment, knowing I could not swim, knowing also I couldn't turn back. I watched him disappear into an opening of trees. Anxious, I followed the shady path to the river's bank. Dark shadows cut across the slow-moving water as my uncle's naked body dove into the river, making a loud plop of a sound. He disappeared, surfaced, floating easily.

The psychology of a river cannot be confined to its banks. I learned to be vulnerable, naked, fearful with the knowledge I could get through to the other side. I learned to trust an adult male to keep me afloat, something my father could not do.

However, I did not learn to swim.

Two artists, Steven Yazzie and Kade Twist, are partners in an American Indian artist collective named Postcommodity. This multidisciplinary, intertribal collective probes the conceptual space of global societies and has realized projects as far afield as Prague. With all the tropes of the contemporary art industry, the collective is pushing hard into the mainstream with an ambitious agenda. It's stretching the reach of a contemporary aesthetic in much the same way as the postcolonial exhibition *Magiciens de la terre* in Paris in 1989. But the real experiment is whether the collective will subsume individual expression. Both artists exhibit distinct works in this exhibition.

The Way the Sun Rises over Rivers Is No Different Than the Way the Sun Sets over Oceans, a new media installation by Twist, is an exploration through video, sound, and text of the Cherokee diaspora and urban Indian experience. Critiquing himself, Twist has written, "Poetry and noise address urban Indian experiences of isolation, familial and clan displacement, economic and political disenfranchisement, substance abuse, and the pervasive hope of returning 'home.' [My work] embeds American Indian geopolitical narratives within a contemporary landscape of American popular culture and consumerism."[13]

In 2006, prompted by a residency at Skowhegan, Steven Yazzie walked out on figurative painting temporarily and began a personal exploration of installation and new-media work. *Sleeping with Jefferson* takes place in present-day Phoenix. The Phoenix metro area is dominated by cars and asphalt and concrete roadways that slice up the landscape. Alongside these "asphalt veins" are ethnic population clusters, "empty lots, mismanaged urban development, and a broken social fabric."[14] The shimmering chrome surface of Yazzie's installation, alive with projected light, masks the impact of homelessness, displacement, and loss of a collective sense of place.

The airplane banks to the left, shivers a moment in hesitation, drops toward the ascending winter-gray earth of the Oklahoma landscape. Southwest flight 3659 on its final approach to the Tulsa International Airport. I think of the wool topcoat I couldn't find at home before I left Phoenix. The airplane seems suddenly colder. I think of the long-ago distant past of a life lived in Oklahoma. I move closer into myself, thinking of the morning light and the highway that will carry me north to home. Trying to come home—it's not an easy thing.

A gray landscape swirled around me. The rental car moved roughly over the broken concrete of Choctaw Avenue and the parking lot of Forest Manor Nursing Home. I looked down at the fragile roses, white with a faint pinkish rim. They seemed cold in the winter landscape. I wanted color. Goddamn small town. There is nothing here except everything we were. Everything we could remember. I took a deep breath of fresh air and punched in the security code that would open the exterior doors. Disinfectant smells rushed outward in the morning air. Low cries of aged souls moved upward into the trees. I kept my eyes level and moved quickly down the hallways toward her room.

She lay in her bed looking down into herself, suspended in some timeless space, waiting for her own journey home. "Aunt Betty, it's Joe Baker." Stirred by a voice,

Kade Twist
The Way the Sun Rises over Rivers
Is No Different Than the Way the
Sun Sets over Oceans, 2007
Media installation
Courtesy of the artist

there is only earth
without mediation

ᏔᏫ ᏤᏣᎦ

of one horizon
or another

Steven Yazzie
Sleeping with Jefferson, 2007
Hubcaps, light projections
183 x 275 x 122 cm.
Courtesy of the artist

her eyes lifted upward into mine. "Why Joe, why didn't you send me a Christmas card? I've been so worried about you. I didn't know what might have happened." I saw my aunt as I have always known her, animated. I apologized, thinking myself a selfish shit to have been too absorbed in my own life to send a card.

"Why have you come home, Joe?" I didn't want to tell her of the interview with the Philbrook. I dodged, making some lame excuse about just wanting to be home. "Joe, that's not why you are here." Her eyes narrowed with interest as I told her of the upcoming interview. Her hand reached out for mine, "Oh Joe, I sure hope this works out, but don't be too disappointed if it doesn't. Just remember, you're not one of them."

Marsha stood in the doorway of her office. My eyes slowly recognized her after twenty years, she as slowly recognized me. Her white suit seemed out of scale for her small frame. She was weighted to the ground, held in place by the palatial walls of her self-created kingdom. Executive director, she reigned. I responded with the finesse born of a six-year rehearsal, remembering all the answers to all the questions hurled at me from the halls of academe. I knew the drill. High atop the Philtower Building in downtown Tulsa, we dined at the Summit Club. Nothing had changed, yet nothing was the same. Marsha ordered and reordered and sent back and tasted and fussed and complained about the limited wine selection as five members of the search committee fired off questions. She stared at me as I stared back at her, a moment of recognition. Two separate worlds never to cross over.

It is my hope that *Remix* will serve as a new working space for imaginative formations—a laboratory for discoveries in indigenous contemporary art that spark new artistic interventions. A place of unexpected encounters. A space in-between the expected. My mind on beginnings, then, I am lost in the search for a conclusion. Perhaps the appropriate thought has already been expressed by the artist Walter Anderson: "Life, you know, is like light. It is continuous. It is our eyes that seek beginnings and endings. I was trying to find an ending with my pencil, but all I found was that there was no ending."[15]

ELEANOR HEARTNEY

Native Identity in an Age of Hybridity

Native Americans occupy a unique place in American culture: as heirs of a troubled history, they often find themselves represented by simplistic and often conflicting stereotypes and myths. In Hollywood movies and popular culture, indigenous people are generally either romanticized as noble savages or vilified as bloodthirsty, firewater-drinking "Injuns." Representations like James Earle Fraser's sculpture *End of the Trail,* an early-20th-century depiction of a doomed and tragic brave slumped on his horse; the embattled Lakota Sioux of Kevin Costner's 1990 film *Dances with Wolves;* or, more recently, the brutal Mayans in Mel Gibson's *Apocalypto* permeate American consciousness and underlie public perceptions about Native Americans. Nor are more serious thinkers immune from such conventions. In her book *The Lure of the Local,* art critic Lucy Lippard contrasts shortsighted, greedy, non-place-oriented "Euro-Americans" with indigenous Americans, who, she argues, place little stake in possessions or borders and practice a more holistic nomadic land ethic. Noting that contemporary Native Americans exist between the two worlds represented by the city and the reservation, she asserts, "This is not to say that the reservation is frozen in the past, but that the present time and space are, from some reports, perceived differently there, in rhythms with the land or in dissonances formed by dissimilarity. Despite casinos and tax havens, the reservation . . . is a symbol of all the land previously occupied or seasonally traveled."[1]

As Lippard herself acknowledges, the danger in these kinds of generalizations is that they threaten to freeze Native Americans into what ethnographer James Clifford refers to as the "ethnographic present." This is a state that fixes ethnographic groups within the traditions that existed before the disruptions caused by the incursions of modernity. Such romanticized formulations ignore or diminish the adjustments Native Americans have made and the transformations they have undergone in partaking of the complexities of contemporary American society. It also threatens to strip Native identity from those who have moved too far from Native traditions.

Hector Ruiz
Vices, 2006
Block print, acrylic, and ink on paper
152 x 102 cm.
Courtesy of an anonymous lender

Clifford has made a case study of one such struggle in his essay "Identity in Mashpee." Here he examines the circumstances around a lawsuit designed to establish whether a contemporary group of individuals calling themselves the Mashpee tribe in Cape Cod, Massachusetts, could be identified with a tribe of the same name that lost its land through contested legislative acts in the mid 19th century. At stake was a very desirable slice of real estate, and at issue was whether individuals of mixed ancestry who had largely assimilated into the non-Indian world could still claim to be Native Americans. As Clifford notes, "Indians in Mashpee owned no tribal lands (other than fifty-five acres acquired just before the trial). They had no surviving language, no clearly distinct religion, no blatant political structure. Their kinship was much diluted. Yet they did have a place and a reputation. For centuries Mashpee had been recognized as an Indian town."[2] Clifford reports on the complex trial proceedings, showing how they reveal the difficulty in pinpointing the essence of Native identity. In the end, the Mashpee's petition was denied, but without resolving the larger questions it raised.

Clifford's essay is a close reading of a much larger phenomenon. In recent years descendants of numerous groups of "involuntary Americans" have won various legal battles to regain some degree of sovereignty over their lands and control over their cultural patrimony. Questions about who is "authentically" Native (and thus a beneficiary of these determinations) are complicated, however, by both U.S. and tribal laws that may, as in the Mashpee case, have conflicting rules about who may be considered a tribal member. Recently, in a decision that provoked charges of discrimination, the Cherokee Nation voted to exclude from membership in the tribe the descendants of the African American slaves held by Cherokees (this despite the fact that petitioners' tribal ancestry was confirmed by the Dawes Rolls, the federal government's list of tribal members living on Cherokee lands in Oklahoma in 1900). At stake in this conflict are not only material benefits, like subsidized health care and housing, but also a sense of self.

Remix represents an effort to move beyond the obsession with Native identity and authenticity. The fifteen artists represented here belong to a younger generation whose self-awareness has been shaped as much by popular culture, movies, music, and literature as by tribal traditions and customs. These artists also represent an inescapable reality of contemporary life, namely the hybrid nature of all identity. Many of them claim double, or even triple, identities, and their artwork tends more toward postmodern strategies like appropriation, deconstruction, and irony than toward assertions of ethnicity or invocations of tribal custom. Even when these artists do touch on such issues, they often do so in a way that throws definitions of "Indianness" into doubt. In this, they reflect a larger discomfort within the contemporary art world with what became known in the 1990s as "identity art." Identity art grew out of demands by marginalized groups for inclusion in the mainstream culture. At its best, identity-based art forced a recognition of the truly multicultural nature of American society. But it also tended to encourage a self-limiting embrace of "otherness," victimhood, and the tropes of cultural authenticity.

Hector Ruiz
41 Shots, 2007
Wood, paint
112 x 51 x 28 cm.
Courtesy of Mimi and
David Horwitz

God of War, 2007
Wood, paint
183 x 61 x 20 cm.
Courtesy of Treg Bradley

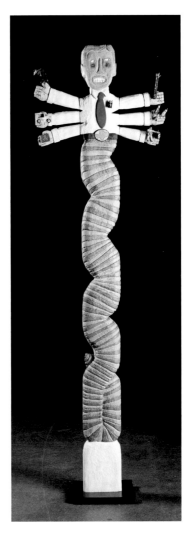

The artists in *Remix* resist such claims in favor of a more promiscuous approach to art and identity. They express a fluid sense of identity, which affirms that there is no such thing as ethnic purity. Instead, as "post Indians," they embrace a reality in which identity is constantly being reshaped by surrounding circumstances. Freedom from the quest for purity allows them to address a diverse set of issues in a wide range of media. This can be seen in the way that several of the artists here rework traditional artistic forms to express their hybrid reality, while others among the fifteen directly address the stereotypes, myths, and historical clichés that surround Native American identity.

Hector Ruiz is an example of the former. He notes that he has lived in two countries (Mexico and the United States) with three identities (Mexican, Kickapoo, and American). He puts all these affiliations into play in works that draw on a range of styles to reflect on the social conditions of those who live on the margins of mainstream society. In his hand-carved sculptures, he uses the idiom of Mexican folk art to create figures that exemplify some of the darker aspects of contemporary American life. For instance, *41 Shots,* a sculpture of a dark-skinned man peppered with holes, memorializes Amadou Diallo, the unarmed African immigrant who

died in a hail of bullets shot by New York City police. *God of War* presents a twist
on Buddhist depictions of Avalokiteshvara, goddess of compassion, in order to
satirize the militaristic tendencies that underlie the carnage of the Iraq War. Ruiz's
prints and paintings draw on the raw emotionalism of German expressionism to
create similarly pointed social commentaries. *Vices* comments on the seductions of
alcoholism, a particular scourge in many Native communities, while *Exposing the
Foundation* meditates on the poorly rewarded and often forgotten groups—among
them Africans, Mexicans, Chinese, and Native Americans—whose labor built
America.

Luis Daniel Gutierrez is Mesa-born, London-educated, and currently lives in
Phoenix. His paintings mingle references to popular culture, Chicano life, and
Mexican folk and religious art. Figures like Batman, Shiva, and the Virgin of
Guadalupe, as well as characters from the artist's life, waft through these colorful
works. Figures are set against flat grounds in iconic poses that recall *retablos* or
tarot cards. Sometimes they are surrounded by skulls, crowns, scissors, or other

Luis Gutierrez
Hank Williams Was a Mexican,
2005
Acrylic on canvas
89 x 74 cm.
Courtesy of Portland's
Restaurant

symbols that bear on the scene depicted. On occasion, written commentaries are scrawled above the figures like graffiti or text bubbles from comics. Many of the works deal with Gutierrez's struggles with multiple sclerosis. *She Must Be Speaking to the Spirits* pays homage to his birth mother, who also suffered from MS and spent the last fifteen years of her life in a nursing home, unable to speak. This work mixes references to birth, life, and death to suggest both the difference and the continuity between mother and son. *Hank Williams Was a Mexican* is a portrait of the country music star. Darkening his skin, Gutierrez emphasizes the kinship he feels with this musician, who, of course, is not actually Mexican. The work is also a sly aside about immigration policies that target Mexicans as undesirables. *Voodoo Lives for Your Pins* is a self-portrait of the artist pierced by pins and hypodermic needles, suggesting a similarity between the ritual piercing of voodoo and the painful injections that are part of the treatment of his disease.

Gregory Lomayesva, whose heritage is both Hopi and Hispanic, also turns to painting to express a very personal vision of the world. He has borrowed from pop

Gregory Lomayesva
The Art of War (sun tzu), 2007
Acrylic on canvas
229 x 229 cm.
Courtesy of the artist

and folk art as well as traditional Hopi imagery, shifting deftly between styles to express different emotional states. The work on display in *Remix* consists of nine paintings meant to be read as a group. They touch on universal subjects like love and loss, but are open to interpretation by the viewer. The images here range from hopeful depictions of emotional connection—a newly wedded couple, and a moment of whispered intimacy—to darker and more disturbing images of fire and destruction. In between are more introspective moments—a woman smoking, a recumbent naked woman. Reflecting on this sequence of images, Lomayesva asks, "Is this a commentary on the social dynamic of love or is it a personal diary of events survived and witnessed or is it the state of delusional creativity where art imitates life, or rather, life imitating art?"[3] He leaves the answer in the viewer's hands.

Another approach to post-Indian identity taken by artists in this show is the re-examination of history as the product of the interplay of fact and myth. For Native Americans, mythology looms large, touching on every aspect of their ancestry. Kent Monkman, who is Cree, produces satirical paintings that bring out the often perverse eroticism latent in pop culture representations of the relationship between Native Americans and the European frontiersmen who displaced them. His invented alter ego is Miss Chief Share Eagle Testickle, a half-breed, drag queen observer of the customs of Native tribes during the great dispersals of the 19th century, and the purported creator of these works.

Si je t'aime, prends garde à toi (If I love you, beware) is a conflation of two iconic art works—James Earle Fraser's 1915 *End of the Trail* and Jean Léon Gérôme's 1882 *Pygmalion and Galatea*. Monkman takes parodic aim at the romanticism with which

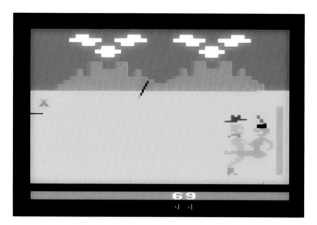

Alan Natachu
Playing NDN, 2006
Video installation
178 x 94 x 91 cm.
Courtesy of the artist

such works deal with the "other." Here Gérôme's Greek sculptor is replaced by a modern-day Lothario who brings a marble version of Fraser's doleful Indian to life with a kiss. Above hovers a cupid whose head has been replaced by a Native American mask. In this and other works in this series, Monkman gives a homoerotic overtone to the ultra-macho mythology of the American West, while awarding the Native American an upper hand in the power dynamics of his cross-cultural scenario.

Alan Natachu turns to modern technology to undermine the Hollywood mythology about Native life. His ongoing project, *Playing NDN*, will eventually take the form of interactive video games that deconstruct the clichéd Native American characters currently available to game players. For *Remix*, he presents a video-game-arcade cabinet in which he has installed a set of videos that are based on conventional games, but that satirize stereotypes such as the bloodthirsty Indian warrior and the sexually voracious Indian woman. This work makes use of Natachu's investigations into the history of video games and the various ways they have shaped the public understanding of Native Americans. By using video games as a medium, he seeks to infiltrate a particularly pervasive and influential form of contemporary entertainment and turn it to his own purposes.

Anna Tsouhlarakis, a Navajo, challenges stereotypes through role reversal. Her video *Let's Dance!* is based on a performance in which she asked people identified with other ethnic traditions to teach her their native dances. The video shows her struggling and sometimes succeeding at learning the very diverse steps of, among other dances, the Irish jig, line dancing, a Bulgarian folk dance, and a Haitian voodoo dance. This joyful work carries echoes of *Funk Lessons*, in which the African American artist Adrian Piper attempted to get a white audience to loosen up and funk dance. Here, however, Tsouhlarakis is the student, rather than the teacher. This allows her to switch places. No longer the ethnic "other" re-enacting her native traditions for the entertainment of curious bystanders, instead she becomes a kind of tourist herself, in the process subtly pointing out that everyone is an "other" to someone else.

Taking a different tack, Franco Mondini-Ruiz, who is a Tejano of Mexican American and Italian stock, challenges dismissive portrayals of two sides of his heritage by humorously embracing them. Deliberately invoking the Mexican vendor of tchotchkes and the Indian trader with his crafts spread out on a blanket in the Indian market, Mondini-Ruiz takes a frankly entrepreneurial approach to the business of art. He churns out massive numbers of saleable objects—pint-sized piñatas in the shape of Western art masterpieces, sculptural assemblages composed of found objects culled from *botanicas*, souvenir shops, and thrift stores; and small paintings (whose price has risen from ninety-nine to 400 dollars apiece as the artist has become better known). For *Remix*, he presents a collection of eight-by-ten-inch canvases that make punning references to high art and contemporary culture.

This project, which Mondini-Ruiz has dubbed *Counterpoint*, playfully displays an anthropological interest in the milieu of the wealthy collectors who frequent art museums and buy art. Here, the cunning Indian vendor hopes to infiltrate their homes with his humble wares. In the process, Mondini-Ruiz, like Tsouhlarakis, turns the tables, reversing the gaze that is usually directed from the privileged Anglo audience toward the exotic "other." Here, the "other" to be scrutinized becomes the class of collectors themselves.

Nadia Myre, who is of Algonquin and French Canadian descent, reveals ambivalence about the Native label. Some of her works trade on iconic Native artifacts, as when she and various collaborators erased the text of the Canadian Indian Act, which defines tribal status, by covering a copy of the document with beads. Others are more personal—poetic—and less moored to issues of identity. Myre has contributed works in both these veins to *Remix*. *Portrait in Motion* is a video documenting a performance in which she paddles a canoe, which she herself created, toward the viewer. The canoe has two halves. The back is traditional birch bark, signifying romantic fantasies about

Nadia Myre
History in Two Parts, 2002
Birch bark, cedar, ash, spruce
root & gum, aluminum
427 x 123 x 91 cm.
Courtesy of the Centre for
Contemporary Canadian Art
© Nadia Myre/licensed by
SODART, Montréal, and
VAGA, New York

Spit of Experience, 2004
Felt and thread
232 x 27 x 27 cm.
Courtesy of Galerie Art Mûr
© Nadia Myre/licensed by
SODART, Montréal, and
VAGA, New York

Canada's First Nations, and the front aluminum, denoting modernity as well as the multi-million-dollar recreational industry. The other work, *Spit of Experience*, is more personal. It is composed of pieces of felt that had a former life as part of an artwork Myre created communally with a group of women at Concordia University in Montréal. The felt has now been rejiggered to create a suspended spire that rests just above the floor and exhibits a gap between its tip and main body. The gap has multiple interpretations, suggesting the silence between words, the space electrical energy must leap to make a connection, or the distance between mind and body.

Bernard Williams, who is the product of a mix of African American and Native ancestry, takes on the sweep of American history with an ever-changing wall installation titled *Charting America*. This work, which Williams alters with each new showing, is composed of cut-out wooden symbols drawn from diverse sources that include American folk art and outsider art, popular culture, cartography, and advertising. In particular, Williams is interested in the American frontier, and the many, often unrecognized cultures and groups that participated in its development. There are references in this monumental work to African American cowboys and soldiers, African American and Indian relations, as well as the mix of Anglos, Hispanics, African Americans, and Asians who made the West their home. Williams also chronicles changes in technology and means of transportation—one can find symbols of the stagecoach, locomotive, automobile, airplane, rifle, AK-47, even on up to the television and computer. One can also trace the changing economic basis of the American West from its agricultural roots to the Gold Rush and the rise of the oil industry. Williams's diagram is roughly chronological, and meant to be read from top to bottom and left to right. Beginning with references to the ships and navigation instruments that led to the "discovery" of

Bernard Williams
NFB–Owatonna, 2005
Acrylic on wood
305 x 366 x 122 cm.
Courtesy of the artist

David Hannan
Untitled (the hunt/hunted),
2006–07
Mixed media installation
Courtesy of the artist, in recognition of the generous support
of the Ontario Arts Council

the New World, *Charting America* moves through the initiation of the slave trade, the American Revolution and Civil War, and the cowboy era up to the present. For *Remix*, Williams has also contributed a sculpture based on the ornamentation of architect Louis Sullivan, who drew from spiritual history and the landscape to create an architectural vision of America.

Other artists make reference to long-standing tropes about Native Americans' intimacy with the natural world. Two quite different approaches are offered here. David Hannan is Métis, a mix of Native and French Canadian ancestry. He celebrates a shamanistic sense of the natural world, re-creating animals like coyotes and deer that have powerful symbolic meanings in Native culture. While his sculptures in some ways resemble taxidermied trophies of the sort brought home by hunters, they are created out of very unnatural materials like urethane foam, auto filler, and translucent packing tape. For instance, *Untitled (the hunt/hunted)* presents a cascade of translucent deer and coyotes suspended from the ceiling. In choosing to depict these creatures, Hannan makes reference to their multiple roles in Native myth. The coyote is seen as a trickster, an agent of transformation, even at times an avatar of the Creator. The deer sometimes appears in myth as a shape-shifting woman. In Hannan's hands these animals become mysterious and ethereal, as if existing somewhere between the worlds of spirit and matter. Meanwhile, their unorthodox materials draw attention to their artificial nature, underscoring the encroachment of technology and urban development on the natural world.

Cherokee artist Kade Twist offers a more elegiac tribute to his tribe's lost connection to nature. In the installation he created for this exhibition, as well as in earlier works, he focuses on the sense of exile felt by Cherokees who were displaced in the 19th century from their original homeland to the Indian Territory in Oklahoma. His contribution to *Remix*, titled *The Way the Sun Rises over Rivers Is No Different Than the Way the Sun Sets over Oceans* deals with a longing to reconnect with the water, and includes video projections of the sun rising over the Illinois River, which runs through the current Cherokee homeland in Oklahoma, and the sun setting over the Pacific Ocean near Los Angeles, site of a later diaspora. The space between these two points exists as a haunting absence, suggesting not only geographical but also psychological distance. An excerpt on the wall from his own writings points out that, "The end of the trail is a moving target." Texts in the Cherokee writing system add another layer to this elegy, as does a sound component that involves found and created sounds, including a Stomp Dance whose rhythms mime the movement of the setting sun.

Other artists examine Native identity through the prism of contemporary life. Dustinn Craig sees an analogy between skateboarding culture and the complexities of traditional tribal life. In his video *4-Wheel Warpony,* he documents the skate-

Dustinn Craig
4-Wheel Warpony, 2007
Video
Courtesy of the artist

Dustinn Craig
4-Wheel Warpony, 2007
Video
Courtesy of the artist

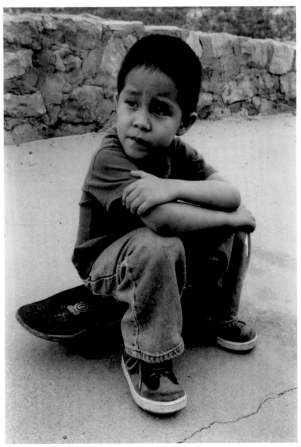

boarding culture of young Apaches, emphasizing the inventiveness of their quest for skateboarding locations, the tight-knit nature of a society whose hierarchy is based on skill, and the web of interconnections with like-minded skateboarding communities elsewhere. Craig, who is himself a skateboarder, notes similarities between efforts to contain skateboarders by providing them with "safe" skating grounds and the effort to domesticate Native tribes by confining them to reservations.

Steven Yazzie, son of a Navajo father and Anglo mother, is interested in the impact of urbanism and automobile culture on contemporary life. His installation, *Sleeping with Jefferson,* uses a formal arrangement of hubcaps floating on water to deal with the population patterns of indigenous peoples in the Phoenix area where he makes his home. The layout of the hubcaps is based on the grid Thomas Jefferson designed in 1785 to make order of the confusing sprawl of the new territories. The artifice of this planning system, which is based on Jefferson's notion of the ideal distribution of land to yeoman farmers, makes it ill-suited to many

Fausto Fernandez
Slip Stitch Symbol, 2007
183 x 208 cm.
Collage: acrylic paint, asphalt
Courtesy of Rand Bradley &
Nathalie Udo

contemporary planning situations, and today its rigid geometric structure gives it sinister overtones of surveillance and coercion. In the context of *Remix*, Yazzie's *Sleeping with Jefferson* also makes reference to the erasure of cultures or individuals who fail to fit into predetermined systems. Projected over the sea of hubcaps is a video of patterns generated by computer models and algorithms, further emphasizing this point.

Fausto Fernandez expresses similar concerns in a very different medium. His delicate, decorative collages are in fact based on other kinds of patterns that control life. Many of these assemblages appropriate blueprints, maps, or sewing patterns into their abstract compositions, allowing the tiny notations and translucent paper to become part of the work. Layered over and between these are curlicues, bands of color, and other flat geometric forms that bring to mind the tradition of modernist abstraction. In fact, however, these also, as in *Slip Stitch Symbol*, may be based on notations that are integral to ordering systems. Fernandez makes an analogy between these mechanical guides and the structuring of human life and behavior, noting that freedom can be an illusion in a society governed by external constraints of law, custom, and history.

Meanwhile, Brian Miller, of Mohawk ancestry, seeks out those areas where freedom, in the form of the unexpected, can still be found. His moody black and white photographs have a cinematic quality, but in fact are records of situations in which he allowed chance and possible danger to take over his life. Some of these works are based on his encounter with a woman on a dark, rural road in New Hampshire, where he now lives. Against his better judgment, he took her home, gave her a place to stay for a few weeks, and photographed her in various environments. The resulting photographs have an eerie quality that captures the nature of his brief relationship with this mysterious stranger. Other works here relate to Miller's equally brief involvement with a religious cult in New Hampshire whose rituals included ingestion of hallucinatory substances. Again, the photographs project an ambience of mystery and inconclusive narrative.

Taken together, the work presented in *Remix* poses an interesting set of questions: What is the meaning of Native identity in a world where mobility, intermarriage, and assimilation have rendered any notion of purity obsolete? Is a life lived in the midst of such flux any less "authentic" than one that adheres to a set of traditions that have been transformed into tourist curiosities? How do history and custom reverberate through the lives of a generation of young artists who refuse to be typecast, but also refuse to abandon essential elements of their past? The title of this exhibition, with its associations with the musical practice of creating alternative versions of an original song through addition, subtraction, alteration of the tempo, or rewriting of the lyrics, presents a provocative model for identity today. In the end, like a remixed song, the important thing about identity isn't how faithful it is to its sources, but how well it plays.

the sun had just set

Noq pay yaw angqe' ima walpeq sinom pay tuwat hiitiita qa pas
aniwnaya. Yaw pumuy uuyiyamuy ima hiitu sowantotaqw oovi yaw
tuho'ostiqw yaw puma qa hiita pas nenngem tunösmaskyatotangwu.
Panmakyangw pu' yaw pay puma nuwu pas oki wtoti. Pay yaw pumuy
oosiwqa'am paapu pa hiisa'hoya pee'iwyungwa.

Introductions: Mixing It Up

"X, I'd like you to meet Y. Y, this is X"—a typical introduction I engage in all the time. No one thinks anything further about it, except perhaps to make conscious note of a name, then ask about work, interests, and so on. This time, however, it was slightly different. I don't want to say that my experience was the first of its kind, and it clearly isn't the last. Encounters like mine now happen routinely throughout Indian Country, and they happen in this book. You see, X has the appearance of an African Canadian, while Y is blond-haired and blue-eyed. Both are confidently Native American. Their meeting wasn't awkward, but rather quite funny. The three of us recognized the irony immediately when I added X's and Y's respective tribes. Looks can be deceiving indeed.

This kind of "racial" moment has been a difficult pill to swallow in the American Indian community, where cultural identity has been so important, and so often focused on appearances. American Express membership has its privileges. Does the same membership principle hold true with American Indians? This question, and the emotional intensity with which it is addressed, are at the core of *Remix*.

Remix came together after a series of discussions with Joe Baker about our working in partnership, he as a curator at the Heard Museum, I , at that time, at the National Museum of the American Indian. These two important institutions were undergoing some radical changes. One of these shifts turned on the proposition that contemporary art practice—guided by artists, critics, and art historians, indigenous and non-indigenous—was advancing the dialogue on art and identity. A good example is a symposium sponsored by NMAI in Venice, Italy, in 2006. That gathering, *Vision Space Desire: Global Perspectives and Cultural Hybridity*, featured artists and intellectuals from across the globe engaged in examining questions very much like those that intrigue the artists in this exhibition. Joe and I both believed that issues and ideas were evolving in a way that would, and should, make people and institutions around the world take notice.

Joe's and my conversation and the symposium in Venice pick up on a historical discussion. Perhaps the last time so many people were thinking about Native art

Gregory Lomayesva
Untitled 1, from *You Can Breathe Now*, 2005
Acrylic on canvas
152 x 152 cm.
Courtesy of the artist

and identity was in 1990, with the passage of the Indian Arts and Crafts Act. The effects of that law, positive and negative, still linger within an older generation of artists. The act itself was written to amend a New Deal law promoting the development of the market for American Indian and Native Alaskan art and handiwork by defining who could sell his of her work with the label "Indian-made." The Indian Arts and Crafts Act has been described as a truth-in-advertising law, but, clearly, issues of identity lie at its core.

It is, of course, the nature of contemporary culture to move on. Native artists quickly raised other—for them, more pressing—concerns centered on contemporary understandings of identity and artistic practice that transcend the intent of the 1990 law. In 1992, Lee-Ann Martin (Mohawk) and I curated *Indigena: Contemporary Native Perspectives in Canadian Art* at the Canadian Museum of Civilization. I remember saying then that an era had come to an end. That era began no later than the opening of the first tourist markets in Southwest, and continued through the *Exposition of Indian Tribal Arts* in Manhattan in 1931, MoMA's *Indian Art of the United States* ten years later, and a number of exhibitions in the 1960s, '70s, and '80s. It was the period when Native artists' work was exhibited only in shows featuring "Indian art," curated by non-Natives. *Indigena* broke the cycle. There would continue to be group shows featuring large casts, but the assumptions had changed. Native artists and curators had finally arrived on something closer to their own terms. Native voices no longer needed to be mediated.

The year 1992 was significant for other reasons. Everyone was set on celebrating the Columbian Quincentenary—everyone, that is, except the Native communities of the Americas. In Canada, a land dispute two years before between the Mohawk Nation and the town of Oka, Québec, had revealed deep fissures between First Nations citizens and non-Native Canadians. That political confrontation, which left three people dead, can be seen as Canada's version of the 1973 standoff at Wounded Knee. It politicized many of us. In 1992, we had no heart for participating in a celebration. Instead, our strategy was to make the public aware of 500 years of injustice toward indigenous peoples. This message motivated us to take curatorial control in *Indigena,* albeit with the support of a museum and museum director, George MacDonald, on-course to catch the shift in the cultural wind.

Why, then, all these years later, would radicalized Native curators continue to organize group shows presenting Native artists? Here, I'd like to cite a concept from anthropology that resonates in the art world: *communitas.* The word refers to the bond formed within a group when its members endure something together as equals, outside the security of the village and its social rules and norms. For example, in some traditional cultures, as part of an initiation ceremony at puberty, boys had to find ways to overcome challenges posed by adults. Often this initiation took place over several days, in very difficult conditions where the boys were isolated from the rest of the community and from the routines of everyday life.

Exploring the idea of solidarity arising from the experience of shared hardship, in 2006 Joe Baker and Lara Taubman curated an exhibition at the Heard entitled *Holy Land: Diaspora and the Desert*. *Holy Land* showed the work of artists from around the world "who share close cultural relationships to desert concepts that engage social, geographical, and psychological issues, [and who] are members of communities that have been displaced by the impact of colonialism and post-colonialism."[1] This kind of thematic exhibition brings together people whose personal and political experiences—by virtue of their differences, as well as their similarities—offer us insights we might not have gained otherwise. A thematic approach has come to characterize many exhibitions originating in artist-run spaces, where artists continually mix and remix. Accustomed to meeting on shared conceptual ground, many younger artists find that related issues, such as borders and boundaries, hybridity, and *métissage*, arise in their work.

In *Remix*, we have created a new communitas—fifteen artists of mixed Native heritage who make great art, but who also explore new ideas and next-level issues. In keeping with the 21st century's embrace of digital media, we asked the artists to document the process of their work through the digital self-portraits that follow. For many Native artists today, cultural identity is not a concern. Nevertheless, we hope that the gathering of this group signifies a new articulation of the expanse and inclusiveness of contemporary Native art.

Fausto Fernandez
Pretty Dated, 2007
183 x 183 cm.
Collage: acrylic paint, spray paint, asphalt
Courtesy of Rand Bradley & Nathalie Udo

Brian Miller
Burnout, 2003
Inkjet print
71 x 112 cm.
Courtesy of the
artist

Dustinn Craig

WHITE MOUNTAIN APACHE/NAVAJO
b. 1975, Mesa AZ
Lives in Mesa AZ
www.4wheelwarpony.com

When the world outside your reservations seems larger than pixels on a screen, your life feels smaller than your little brother. Apache kids with skateboards live with dreams so large they will never dare to tell anyone. Yet those dreams get a little smaller each year, with the death of a friend, or the impossible success of another. This is the story of young Apache men growing into a world they fear will crush them into shame and obscurity. Some of these boys are fathers, alcoholics, dropouts, artists, writers, and poets. Some are dead, ghosts recollected on drunken nights when the world hurts too much to try.

—Dustinn Craig

In one of Dustinn Craig's images, a young hitchhiker stands alongside a lonely stretch of road, thumb stuck out, no car in sight. Is he running from home? We can see a small community in the distance. Dressed in hip-hop style, he carries only a skateboard. Is he going somewhere to realize his dreams or to the next village to see his friends? Some might say he's going nowhere, but Craig would argue with that. "Skateboard culture, like Native culture is often borrowed or stolen, then regurgitated to the public for profit in a distorted form resented by skateboarders. What may seem to be White Mountain Apache youth borrowing 'pop-culture' in place of their own is actually Apache culture of young men manifesting itself within skateboard culture." In fact, skateboarding is so powerful and affirming for these young men that Dustinn Craig's skateboarders remind us of when horses were first introduced into Indian Country. In another series of images, we see 19th-century-style Apache warriors standing squarely in an unmediated landscape. Are they the famous resistors who gave rise to Chief Geronimo? After a series of shots it is revealed that they, too, are skateboarders. With the by-line "Style is king!" the image could pass as the most polished Madison Avenue ad campaign. This reflexivity is appealing to the new generation of Native artists, who shift out of one identity into another with an ease that disconcerts traditionalists. —GM

VIDEOGRAPHY AND SCREENINGS

In production   *Ride through Genocide*

                      Chiricahua Apache Geronimo, for *The American Experience*, 2009

2005   *HOME*, *Havasupai*, and *Colorado River Indian Tribes*, three films for the Heard Museum installation "Native People of the Southwest"

2004   *White Mountain Apache Creation Story*, in Apache with English subtitles, produced for the Fort Apache Museum on the White Mountain Apache Reservation

2003   *Matters of Race*, produced by Roja Productions for PBS

EDUCATION

R.E.Z. University

4 wheel war pony

Fausto Fernandez

MEXICAN/AMERICAN
b. 1975, El Paso TX
Lives in Phoenix AZ
www.faustofernandez.blogspot.com

My work is based on my curiosity of the relationships between people in society and how these relationships impact my personality and life experiences. I believe we live in a society that lacks freedom, where most of the things we do are products of information from outside sources, such as guidelines, laws, procedures, time, and numbers. The blueprints, sewing patterns, and maps in my work represent the guides we follow in our life to create a more stable way to go through daily routines.

—Fausto Fernandez

Fausto Fernandez uses sewing patterns and maps as canvases, from which emerge some of the most exciting and unexpected paintings. His reworking of these familiar objects with paper cut-outs, asphalt, acrylic, and spray paint gives them new, subjective meanings. Australia's first peoples created paintings that combined with songs to guide them through the expansive territories in which they lived. Their maps were no doubt more than spatial, but rather included all that lived within their part of the world. In Fernandez's patterns and maps, too, we see the lyrical. "In relationships there are no formulas or guides to follow," he says. "We create our own methods to create intimacy. I compare the guides and patterns in our daily routines to the methods we use to keep a relationship working."[2]—GM

SOLO EXHIBITION

2007   *Fausto Fernandez*, The Latin American Art Gallery, Scottsdale AZ

SELECTED GROUP EXHIBITIONS

2007   Arizona Biennial '07, Tucson AZ

Grand Opening, The Latin American Art Gallery, Scottsdale AZ

Fausto Fernandez, Hector Ruiz, Glenn Allen, Collin Chillag and Pete Deice, The Chocolate Factory, Phoenix AZ

Fausto Fernandez and Abbey Messmer, Pravus at Anti-Space, Phoenix AZ

2006   *Chaos Theory 7*, Legend City Studios, Phoenix AZ

Archi-Textures: Works by Fausto Fernandez, Toni Gentilli, Scott Murphy, RLV Gallery, Oracle AZ

2005   *Works by Fausto Fernandez, Hector Ruiz, Glenn Allen, Mykil Zep and Rachel Bess*, The Chocolate Factory, Phoenix AZ

2004   *Isn't It Grand*, 3 Car Pile-Up, Phoenix AZ

Valentine's Day Exhibition, Ice House, Phoenix AZ

Art Detour Group Show, Paulina Miller Gallery, Phoenix AZ

Mis.ceg.e.na.tion: A mixture of different races, The Chocolate Factory, Phoenix AZ

Fausto Fernandez, Luis Gutierrez, Kyllan Maney and Ann Tracy-Lopez, Paulina Miller Gallery, Phoenix AZ

EDUCATION

2001   BFA in painting, BFA in graphic design, University of Texas in El Paso, El Paso TX

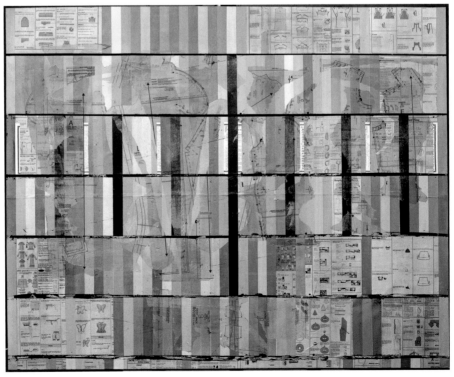

Fausto Fernandez
Adjustment Line for Miss Petite,
2007
183 x 208 cm.
Collage: acrylic paint, asphalt
Courtesy of Rand Bradley &
Nathalie Udo

Luis Gutierrez

MEXICAN/AMERICAN
b. 1969, Mesa AZ
Lives in Phoenix AZ
http://www.luisdanielgutierrez.com

You can't come out with anything if you don't know yourself, and people have to sit down and figure out who they are, constantly, since they are always in flux. I'm an emotional person, and to figure myself out I'll sit down and try to figure out what the hell I'm feeling. Then I think, "If I could sum up how I'm feeling, how would it be?"
—Luis Daniel Gutierrez

While studying in London, Luis Daniel Gutierrez felt his individuality come up against English historical and cultural weight. The cold, gray atmosphere of England made him miss "the Virgin of Guadalupe, low-riders, brown people, and colors" of Phoenix. "In England," he says, "I started drawing bits from my culture. My paintings were only meant to comfort me and were never shown to my instructors at school or in an exhibition. Then I came back to the U.S. and realized that was my work. It was like a homecoming, and those little drawings, those were my work." Since then, Gutierrez's art has branched out to include three-dimensional compositions. "I want to go and collect the immigrants' trash at the border and make saints out of it. I want to talk about how people with nothing can and do make the seemingly impossible, possible. I am also directing my painting at 'discovering' the masters of Old World Europe. My premise is to find out what would have happened if a Native American discovered Europe rather than the way it has played out."[3]—GM

SELECTED EXHIBITIONS

2007 *Phoenix Showcase*, Himeji, Japan
   Chem Lab, Phoenix AZ
   Portland's Cafe Royale, Phoenix AZ
2006 Paper Heart Art Space, Phoenix AZ
   Stop and Look Gallery, Phoenix AZ
2005 Cone Gallery, Phoenix AZ
   Museo Chicano, Phoenix AZ
2004 The Chocolate Factory, Phoenix AZ
2003 Espresso Depot, Phoenix AZ
2002 *This-Ability*, 50th Anniversary of the Berlin Multiple Sclerosis Society,
    Berlin, Germany

EDUCATION

1992 BA, Richmond University, London

David Hannan

MÉTIS
b. 1971, Ottawa ON
Lives in Toronto ON
home.the.wire.com/~dhannan

I am a Métis artist whose image content has developed from research into written histories of the Métis, as well as from less formal sources such as friends and family, in the oral tradition. In this work I have tried to tackle some of the complex issues surrounding contemporary Métis and their relationship to the Canadian landscape. My relationship to the land is obviously important, but is continually changing, and does not rely on old stereotypes that have been perpetuated by many artists in the past. This installation shows us that the relationship to the land is quickly becoming more and more urbanized, entangled between traditional life and adapting and living in an urban society.

—David Hannan

David Hannan's sculptures have a social aspect to them. Big-game hunters and natural scientists capture nature for their own reasons—pride, in the hunter's case, a wish to study the world in a certain way, in the scientist's. Mounted trophies and type specimens hold different meanings for Native people. For natural history museums throughout the world—including in the United States and Canada—dioramas populated with mannequins of aboriginal groups appear to be no more problematic than taxidermic displays of wild animals. Hannan's hybrid creatures can be seen equally as metaphors for his Canadian Métis identity. The concept of *métissage*—of mixed ethnicity and culture—has now become standard discourse, a new identity for a post-Indian (post-race) world. This stands in contrast to even the recent past, when society seemed to insist on some kind of racial or cultural "authenticity." Hannan's sculpture *Untitled (the hunt/hunted)* is nonetheless disturbing, very much like the work of Australian sculptor Patricia Piccinini, who similarly questions notions of normality. In her work we see the mixing of animal and human features and characteristics in a kind of genomic experiment. Hannan keeps his animals animals, but crowds them together in ways that emphasize their bodies. For this installation Hannan's suspended deer and coyotes rotate on a fan. There's no sense of fear in their fall, nor do they appear as carcasses ready for slaughter. It is as though they are diving down from a skyworld, not quite hitting the earth. —GM

SELECTED SOLO EXHIBITIONS

2006   *ALLcreatures*, Gallery 101, Ottawa ON
2004   *DOUBLEcurve*, Thunder Bay Art Gallery, Thunder Bay ON
2004   *David Hannan new works*, Galerie St. Laurent + Hill, Ottawa ON

SELECTED GROUP EXHIBITIONS

2005   *Everyday Light*, Thunder Bay Art Gallery, Thunder Bay ON
2004   *Utopia/ Dystopia*, York Quay Gallery Case Studies, Toronto ON

PUBLIC COLLECTIONS

National Aboriginal Achievement Foundation, Ohsweken ON
Thunder Bay Art Gallery, Thunder Bay ON
Indian Art Centre, Indian and Northern Affairs Canada, Hull QC
Woodland Cultural Centre, Brantford ON

EDUCATION

1995   AOCA diploma with honors, Ontario College of Art, Toronto ON

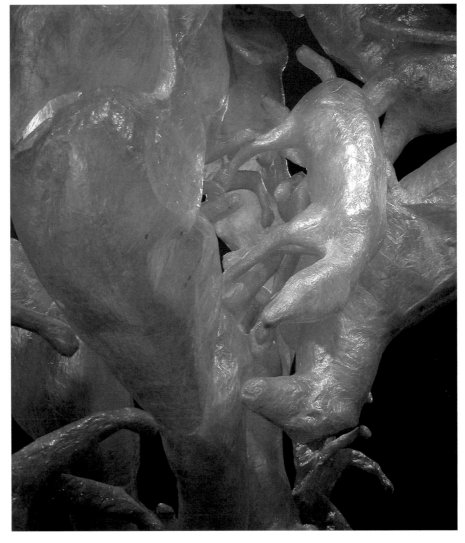

Gregory Lomayesva

HOPI/HISPANIC
b. 1971, Phoenix AZ
Lives in Santa Fe NM
www.lomayesva.com

Everything I do is based in this merging of styles and backgrounds: pop art with Spanish art, Native art with surrealism, images I find in Vogue with folk legends my mom has told me. Still, you're always kind of bound by "the assumption," by other people's assumptions.

—Gregory Lomayesva

The son of a Hopi father and a Hispanic mother, both accomplished artists, Gregory Lomayesva grew up experientially, if not geographically, far from the Hopi Nation. His yearning for attachment has come at a cost. Of his early art—masks and "katsina-type" dolls—he says, "Some Hopis said my work was sacrilegious. Because I wasn't born on the reservation, I didn't know the rules. They could criticize my non-conformity, but they couldn't take my last name or my heritage from me. Nonetheless it was a slap on my face that really hurt. I was still coming to terms with my feelings of being really Indian, and the last thing I needed was the burden of guilt." Since then, the symbolism in his work has become increasing personal and ekphrastic—combining sculpture or images and poetic language. In Lomayesva's series of paintings *You Can Breathe Now* (2005), houses burn, yet there is a troubling presence of life, signified by the light through the windows and doors. The images leave us with questions not only of what we are witnessing, but of what the written text—part Hopi, part English—is about. His work for *Remix*, *The Art of War (sun tzu)*, again puts us in the position of witnesses. The story, this time told without words, is no less compelling.[4] —GM

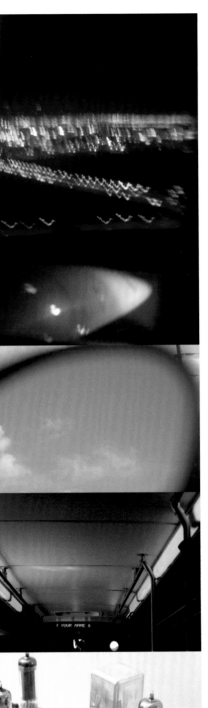

SELECTED SOLO EXHIBITIONS

2006   *More Indian*, Winterrowd Fine Art, Santa Fe NM
         The Art of War, Art and Industry, Santa Fe NM
2005   *You Can Breathe Now*, J. Cacciola Gallery, New York NY
         Flutter, Studio Gallery, Washington DC
         Untitled, Chiaroscuro Gallery, Scottsdale NM
2004   *16:9*, Peyton Wright Gallery, Santa Fe NM

SELECTED GROUP EXHIBITIONS

2007   *Unlimited Boundaries*, Albuquerque Museum, Albuquerque NM
2000   *NM2000*, Museum of Fine Arts, Santa Fe NM

EDUCATION

Self-taught after 9th grade

Brian Miller
MOHAWK
b. 1969, Greece NY
Lives in Acworth NH

One night on an empty road in New Hampshire in the fall of 2001, I picked up a woman who was hitchhiking. She proposed that I photograph her in exchange for giving her a place to stay for a few days. The reality became progressively stranger, and couple of days became three and a half weeks. I photographed her incessantly, without thinking. Certain images remind me of Dante's Inferno, his descent into hell. I began to see the old dirt roads and abandoned places of New Hampshire as a modern analog for hell. They now seem to be haunted places.

—Brian Miller

Brian David Kahehtowanen Miller's images of sexual politics are based on a chance meeting with a female hitchhiker who needed a place to stay and, in exchange, agreed to be photographed. The dark, foreboding images of that three-week encounter form a mysterious narrative. Miller's muse is first seen sitting inside a vehicle looking directly at the viewer. We also see her lying on the ground in front of a car that has its lights on. In another instance she purses her lips for the camera, and in another a male hand (Miller's) grabs at her tank top, which has its own mystery. It's never night or day, but somewhere in between, though a faint light flecks through the trees. In the late 1950s and early '60s, there was a well-known television series called *The Twilight Zone*, eerie stories that questioned the unexplained. Similarly Miller's twilight series is all about what lies between, the interstices between light and dark, the conscious and unconscious, fiction and reality. Miller leaves space between the photographs for us to fill with our own thoughts. Invited to build the narrative, we are left only with more questions. —GM

Brian Miller

*Come Back and Bring
Your Temper Boy*, 2003
Inkjet print
71 x 112 cm.
Courtesy of the artist

Wolf, 2003
Inkjet print
71 x 112 cm.
Courtesy of the artist

Preacher's Room, 2003
Ink jet print
71 x 112 cm.
Courtesy of the artist

Trailer Trash, 2003
Inkjet print
71 x 112 cm.
Courtesy of the artist

SELECTED EXHIBITIONS

2008   *Hulleah Tsinhnahjinnie, Nora Naranjo Morse &
            Brian Miller*, Berlin Gallery, Phoenix AZ

2007   *Little Stories*, Berlin Gallery, Phoenix AZ

2006   *Group Exhibition*, Berlin Gallery, Phoenix AZ
        Aldrich Undercover, Aldrich Museum,
            Ridgefield CT
        A Series of Minor Miracles, Raw & Co Gallery,
            Cleveland OH
        50 Year Anniversary Exhibit, Roger Williams
            College, Bristol RI
        Black & White, Holland Tunnel Gallery,
            New York NY

2005   *Selections*, Loco Ritorio Gallery, Boston MA
        Faculty Show, Jaffe-Friede & Strauss Galleries,
            Dartmouth College, Hanover NH

SELECTED PUBLIC COLLECTIONS

Rauner Special Collections Library,
        Dartmouth College, Hanover NH
Heard Museum, Phoenix AZ
Yale University & Yale Art Gallery, New Haven CT
State University of New York, Purchase NY

EDUCATION

1995   MFA, Yale School of Art, New Haven CT
1992   BFA, State University of New York,
            Purchase NY

Franco Mondini-Ruiz

TEJANO/ITALIAN
b. 1961, San Antonio TX
Lives in San Antonio TX
http://www.frederieketaylorgallery.com/artists.html

We're not purely American and, if we go to Mexico, we're not Mexicans, either. We are the American story; we're a hybridization of culture.

—Franco Mondini-Ruiz

In 1995, Franco Mondini-Ruiz left a law career to become an artist, a move that usually happens in reverse. At the 2000 Whitney Biennial in New York, Mondini-Ruiz sold small objects outside the museum, some for as little as ten cents and none for more than ten dollars. Many he decorated on the spot for passersby. The idea of creating affordable art is not new; neither is making small pictures, or bringing art and life together. Mondini-Ruiz's approach to accessibility, portability, and spontaneity, however, defies the clamor for authenticity, for one-of-a-kind preciousness, that reigns in the art world. And his deceptively modest paintings often punch above their weight. In *Cowboys Out of Indians*, we see two tiny figures wearing red shirts, sitting on horses. They seem to be chatting with each other. The title is a truism—making cowboys out of Indians was practically the goal of 19th-century assimilationist policy. Yet had Mondini-Ruiz called his painting the reverse—*Indians Out of Cowboys*—the scene would be a paradox. Cowboy and Indian are not binary or symmetrical identities after all. Mondini-Ruiz seems to use his work to puncture that part of the American dream that needs good guys and bad guys, whether in the Wild West of yesterday or the Middle East of today.[5] —GM

SELECTED SOLO EXHIBITIONS

2008   Frederieke Taylor Gallery, New York NY

2007   Project in conjunction with *Mexicana: Discovering Mexican Popular Arts,*
         1919–1950, Newark Museum of Art, Newark NJ

2006   *Hollywood Squares,* Light Box Gallery, Los Angeles CA

2005   *Quattrocento: 400 Paintings,* Frederieke Taylor Gallery, New York NY
         Postcards from Rome, American Academy in Rome, Italy
         Small Treasures, Projetto Biagiotti, Florence, Italy
         ¡Que Purdy!, New World Museum, Houston TX

2004   *Botanica Los Angeles,* UCLA Fowler Museum, Los Angeles CA
         Giant, Marfa Ballroom, Marfa TX
         99 Paintings, McColl Center for the Arts, Charlotte NC

SELECTED GROUP EXHIBITIONS

2007   *Ulterior Motifs: A Celebratory Art Extravaganza,* Arlington Museum of Art,
         Arlington TX
         The Mexican Museum's Nuevo Arte: Colección Tequila Don Julio,
         traveling exhibition, New York NY

2006   *Transitional Objects: Contemporary Still Life,* Neuberger Museum of Art,
         SUNY Purchase College, Purchase NY

2005   *Infinito Botanica: Bologna,* Bologna Art Fair, Bologna, Italy
         The Prague Biennale, Prague Museum of Contemporary Art, Prague,
         Czech Republic
         Down the Garden Path: The Artist's Garden after Modernism,
         Queens Art Museum, Queens NY

2004   *I Heart Texas,* Allston Skirt Gallery, Boston MA
         Twang, Art Museum of Southeast Texas, Beaumont TX
         Salon Carlotta, McColl Center for the Arts, Charlotte NC
         Half Baked Sales, Frederieke Taylor Gallery, Affordable Art Fair,
         New York NY

2003   *Communities (Mexican Town),* Wayne State University, Detroit MI

BOOK

High Pink: Tex-Mex Fairy Tales, New York:
   DAP/Distributed Arts Publishers, 2005

EDUCATION

1985   JD Law, St. Mary's University
         School of Law, San Antonio TX

1981   BA English, St. Mary's
         University, San Antonio TX

Kent Monkman

CREE/ENGLISH/IRISH
b. 1965, St. Marys ON
Lives in Toronto ON
www.urbannation.com

In my current body of paintings, **The Moral Landscape,** *I appropri-ate the romantic landscapes of 19th-century North American painters such as Albert Bierstadt, Thomas Cole, George Catlin, and Paul Kane to investigate the relationship of sexuality to conquest, xenophobia, and imperialism. In my versions, the familiar players in North American history (Indians, explorers, and cowboys) are reconfigured in pro-vocative and humorous sexual vignettes set against the sublime land-scape. Emulating the context of the original paintings as ethnological documentation, or pictures from a travelogue, my paintings play with power dynamics within sexuality to challenge historical assumptions of sovereignty, art, commerce, and colonialism.*

—Kent Monkman

James Earle Fraser's *End of the Trail* (1915) is an icon of divergent meanings. The sculpture itself—an 18-foot plaster work on view in Oklahoma City's National Cowboy and Western Heritage Museum—shows a tired brave sitting atop his equally weary horse. Fraser's work mournfully conveys the belief, widespread at the turn of the 20th century, that American Indians were in the twilight of their existence. For Fraser, art was a way to preserve their memory. Today Native Americans have appropriated Fraser's overdetermined imagery for our own ends. With his usual flourish, Kent Monkman bases *Si je t'aime, prends garde à toi* in part on Fraser, in part on Jean Léon Gérôme's retelling of the myth of the sculptor who falls in love with his creation (psychologists call an erotic attraction to statues pygmalionism). Monkman, many of whose works redress the invisibility of the gay male in U.S. and Canadian history, paints the cold stone coming to life as Fraser and his warrior kiss. Like Gérôme, Monkman includes a cupid, albeit with the head of the trickster, Raven. Raven appears again as a mask on the background ledge, wearing what seems like a sly, mischievous smile. In the background, too, is a small version of Fraser's sculpture (you can buy one at Sam's Club), as well as warriors' accoutrements apparently collected by the sculptor. At issue is the fine line between representation and reality, between art and life. —GM

SELECTED SOLO EXHIBITIONS

2007 *The Triumph of Mischief*, Art Gallery of Hamilton, Hamilton ON
2007 *Hunting Scenes and Other Amusements from the Great North West*,
      Pierre Francois Ouellette Art Contemporain, Montréal QC
2006 *Kent Monkman*, with essay by Paul Chaat Smith, Walter Phillips Gallery,
      Banff AB

PERFORMANCES

2006 *Gone with the Wind*, Museum of Contemporary Canadian Art,
      Toronto ON
2005 *Share Eagle Testickle: Artist and Model*, Drake Hotel, Toronto ON
      The Taxonomy of the European Male, Compton Verney, Warwickshire UK
2004 *Group of Seven Inches*, McMichael Canadian Art Collection, Kleinburg ON

VIDEOGRAPHY

2006 *Robin's Hood* (currently in post-production)
      Shooting Geronimo
2005 *Group of Seven Inches*

SELECTED GROUP EXHIBITIONS

2007 *Shapeshifters, Time Travellers and Storytellers*, ICC and imagineNative at
      the Royal Ontario Museum, Toronto ON
      Crack the Sky, Montréal Biennale, Centre Internationale d'Art
      Contemporain de Montréal, Montréal QC
2006 *Salon Indien*, Toronto International Art Fair, Toronto ON
2006 *Unholy Alliance: Art and Fashion Meet Again*, Museum of Contemporary
      Canadian Art, Toronto ON
2006 *Re-thinking Nordic Colonialism*, The Nordic Institute for Contemporary
      Art, Helsinki, Finland
2005 *Hot Mush and the Cold North*, Ottawa Art Gallery, Ottawa ON
2005 *The American West*, Compton Verney, Warwickshire UK

SELECTED PUBLIC COLLECTIONS

National Gallery of Canada, Ottawa ON
Musée national des beaux-arts du Québec, Québec City QC
Museum London, London UK
Woodland Cultural Centre, Brantford ON
MacKenzie Art Gallery, Regina SK
Canada Council Art Bank, Ottawa ON

EDUCATION

1989 Diploma, Sheridan College of Applied Arts, Oakville ON

Kent Monkman
Emergence of a Legend, 2007
3 from a series of of 5 digital
prints on metallic paper
16 x 11 cm. each
Courtesy of the artist

Nadia Myre

ANISHINAABE
b. 1974, Montréal QC
Lives in Saint-André d'Argenteuil QC
www.nadiamyre.com

My interests in art making have been predominately focused on the deconstruction of lingual and material languages as a method of understanding. I am equally interested in "the story"—collective memory and wounds—as it relates to the colonization of Anishinaabe people. I move around from mediums in an effort to express my ideas as best I can.

—Nadia Myre

Nadia Myre's sculptures and installations possess the kind of mutation and mixing described as *métissage*. A good example is Myre's *Portrait in Motion*, in which she uses a hybridized canoe form—one-half made from wood and birch bark, the other aluminium—to produce a view of Canadian history as merging European and aboriginal peoples. In *Spit of Experience*, Myre piles rolls of felt of varying sizes one atop another, in a shape reminiscent of the carefully carved layers of meat served in Lebanese take-outs. The word "spit" has several interesting connotations, beyond the rotisserie, that may lead to a better understanding of this work. A spit is land extending out into the water. Perhaps Myre's sculpture is a metaphor for the gradual loss of her people's land through colonial theft by force and the still-controversial treaty process. Then there is the improvisational freestyling or "spitting" in contemporary rap music. Myre offers up meanings, one on top another, with references to tradition, history, memory, or received knowledge from an ancestral past. *Spit of Experience*, then, can be read as referring to our ability to do with our past as we see fit, or the accumulation of experiences that makes up who we are. The singular column becomes a metaphor for our individuality.[6] —GM

VIDEOGRAPHY AND SCREENINGS

2007   *Debt in the Drift*
        Betting on the Bank
2006   *Red Eye*, Carleton University Art Gallery, Ottawa ON
2005   imagineNATIVE Film + Media Arts Festival, Toronto ON
        IMAGeNATION Aboriginal Film and Video Festival, Vancouver BC

2004   *Inkanatatation*
        Your True Love
2002   *Wish*
        Portrait as a River in Motion
        First Peoples' Festival, Montréal QC

SELECTED SOLO EXHIBITIONS

2008   Musée d'art contemporain des Laurentides, St. Jérome QC
        Sabotage: A Series of Possible Outcomes, Art Mûr, Montréal QC
2006   *The Want Ads and Other Scars*, Urban Shaman, Winnipeg MB
        The Scar Project, Third Space Gallery, Saint John NB
2004–05 *Cicatrices: histoires partagées*, Art Mûr, Montréal, QC
        Skin Deep, or Poetry for the Blind / Cicatrices, ou poésie pour les aveugles,
            Union Gallery, Queen's University, Kingston ON, and Art Mûr,
            Montréal QC

SELECTED GROUP EXHIBITIONS

2007   *Here We Gather: Aboriginal Perspectives on Time and Space*, Royal Ontario
            Museum–Crystal Gallery, Toronto ON
        In My Lifetime, Canadian Museum of Civilization, Hull QC
        Making Real, hosted by the National Arts Centre for the Québec Arts
            Scene, TD Bank on Sparks Street, Ottawa ON
2006   *Fray*, The Textile Museum and the Koffler Gallery, Toronto ON
        Making Sense of Things, McMaster Museum of Art, Hamilton ON, and the
            Gorman Art Gallery, University of California, Davis CA
        Making Sense of Things, Gorman Art Gallery, University of California,
            Davis CA
2005   *The American West*, Compton Verney Gallery, Warwickshire UK
        Nouvelles acquisitions de la COPA, Musée national des beaux-arts du
            Québec, Québec QC
        In My Lifetime, Musée national des beaux-arts du Québec, Québec QC

SELECTED PUBLIC COLLECTIONS

Canadian Museum of Civilization, Hull QC
Eiteljorg Museum, Indianapolis IN
Galerie Art Mûr, Montréal QC
Indian Art Centre, Ottawa ON
Musée national des beaux-arts du Québec, Québec QC
National Aboriginal Achievement Foundation, Ohsweken ON
Woodland Cultural Centre, Brantford ON

EDUCATION

2002   MFA in sculpture, Concordia University, Montréal QC
1997   Diploma, Emily Carr School of Art, Vancouver BC
1995   AFA, Camosun College, Victoria BC

Alan Natachu

ZUNI/LAGUNA
b. 1980, Zuni NM
Lives in Madison WI
www.playingndn.net (launches fall 2007 for *Remix*)

Up, Up, Down, Down, Left, Right, Left, Right, B, A, Start. Video games no longer are associated with the stigma of being child's play. They have made their way from dissipated arcades to the main rooms of the household, often sitting next to the modern day storytellers of DVD players and satellite dish receivers. Playing NDN is derived from many caffeine-laced nocturnal adventures involving flashing pixels, automated beeps, and the never-ending quest for extra lives. This work is my attempt to examine the portrayal of the Native American motif in console video games.

—Alan Natachu

In the age of tribal casinos and splashy Indian cultural centers, along comes a young artist who uses a pop-culture medium as glittering and tawdry as anything in Las Vegas—the video game. Alan Natachu, a recent graduate of the Institute of American Indian Arts, takes the burdensome "Indian" characters offered by mass entertainment and makes superheroes of them. Superheroes are nothing new in Indian Country, from the culture heroes of our origin stories to Super Shamou, the Baker Lake Inuk Superman created by Barney Pattunguyak and Peter Tapatai for the Inuit Broadcasting Corporation in 1987. Natachu responds to the debate over who or what a real Indian is, and how a real Indian should behave, with ethnic essentialism. He has taken the pan-Indian cultural stereotypes that lie beneath these questions and turned them to his own purposes. After all, cheering for an antihero is better than forever being on the losing side (which is why for years we cheered for cowboys). A New Mexico newspaper columnist writes that Natachu, "with his long, shiny braids and dapper red-and-black saddle shoes, is the definition of Native culture mixing with a new direction." Is this also what Natachu intends his heroes to represent?[7] —GM

SELECTED SCREENINGS

2006　Haskell University, Lawrence KS

2005　Heard Museum, Phoenix AZ

El Morro Theater, Gallup NM

University of New Mexico Albuquerque NM

Santa Fe Film Festival, Santa Fe NM

2003–05　Institute of American Indian Arts Museum, Santa Fe NM

2003　Denver Art Museum, Denver CO

EDUCATION

2005　BFA in creative writing, Institute of American Indian Arts, Santa Fe NM

2002　AFA in creative writing, Institute of American Indian Arts, Santa Fe NM

Alan Natachu
Playing NDN, 2006
Video installation
Courtesy of the artist

Hector Ruiz

KICKAPOO/MEXICAN/AMERICAN
b. 1971, Houston TX
Lives in Phoenix AZ

All my life I have lived in a border state. I have lived with the reality of an ethnic, cultural, and very real racial border between my people. In my work, I explore the bicultural paradoxes and multiracial visions and expos of the Eurocentric community and country I live in. Culture is without borders, but once mixed with Western culture, it is about change.

—Hector Ruiz

Hector Ruiz spent his childhood in Eagle Pass, Texas, and Piedras Negras, Mexico, before moving with his family to Austin, Texas. Living near the border has shaped his worldview and identity. In the American Southwest, Ruiz sees principles of liberty stretched to the breaking point by a discourse that institutionalizes racism, or, at best, pits Americans against Mexicans. As a Mexican Indian, he changes the discourse, and shakes up the simplistic white-brown dichotomy. His commitment to self-expression and the community of artists has led him to invite artists from throughout the United States to the Chocolate Factory, his studio/gallery in Phoenix, where they are free to do their own thing, whether that means installations, performances, or making art for sale. Ruiz's own work, which draws on the folk- and fine-art traditions of Mexico, Latin America, and Native America, is rooted in his reverence for the past and for other cultures, and has been shaped by travel. He notes, for example, that in the United States, people from south of the border are treated much like gypsies in Europe: they have no land, no treaties, no commodifiable Native culture. Though his art seems political, he is more interested in prodding people to examine the realities around them.[8] —GM

SELECTED SOLO EXHIBITIONS

2007   *New Works*, Bentley Gallery, Scottsdale AZ

2006   *The Standard*, Bentley Projects, Phoenix AZ

2005   *La Realidad*, Heard Museum, Phoenix AZ

2004   *Manifest Destiny*, LoDo/PCCA, Phoenix AZ

SELECTED GROUP EXHIBITIONS

2005   *Identity: Divided Transformations*, Phoenix College, Phoenix AZ

2005   *Chaos Theory*, Legend City, Phoenix AZ

       Displaced, The Chocolate Factory, Phoenix AZ

       $100 Group Show, LoDo/PCCA, Phoenix AZ

2004   *Miscegenation*, The Chocolate Factory, Phoenix AZ

       Group Show, Icehouse, Phoenix AZ

       Faculty Show, Rudy and Wanda Turk Galleries, Tempe AZ

       Art Detour Group Show, Icon Gallery, Phoenix AZ

PUBLIC COLLECTION

Heard Museum, Phoenix AZ

EDUCATION

1994   BFA, Arizona State University, Tempe AZ

Anna Tsouhlarakis

NAVAJO/CREEK/GREEK
b. 1977, Lawrence KS
Lives in Washington DC
www.naveeks.com

There are certain perceptions and expectations that make an artwork fit into the confines of Native American art. In my work, I try to challenge and stretch those boundaries to their fullest potential. I create pieces that reveal a truth that has been hidden or neglected. The realm of Native America is full of romanticism and spirituality. Unfortunately most Native American art is held to that same limitation and therefore has remained stagnant. I question why those limitations transfer to the gallery setting and why they have maintained their presence for so long.

—Anna Tsouhlarakis

Anna Tsouhlarakis speaks in the international language of dance, in which participation is key. *Let's Dance!* reminds me of the late 1970s disco era, when a string of hits catapulted Donna Summer to stardom. They were fun songs for a liberated time. Similarly, Tsouhlarakis has created a concept album for a new modernity, and reinterpreted the association between Indians and dancing. In *Let's Dance!*, a video done over a period of thirty days while she was an artist-in-residence at the Skowhegan School in Maine, Tsouhlarakis dances with thirty partners, each of whom contributes a different dance. The results are amazing. Somehow Tsouhlarakis manages to say that dance is both ethnic and for everyone. And although the universality of dance is the central image, it would be a mistake to overlook the humor in Tsouhlarakis's work. She reveals dance as serious business loaded with goodwill. —GM

SOLO EXHIBITIONS

2007   *Clash of the Titans II*, Navajo Nation Museum, Window Rock AZ
           Clash of the Titans, American Indian Community House Gallery,
              New York NY

2005   *fixations*, Downtown Contemporary Art Center, Albuquerque NM

SELECTED GROUP EXHIBITIONS

2007   *The New York Armory Show*, New York NY
           Conservation and Construction: The Evolution of the American Landscape,
              Gallery RFD, Swainsboro GA

2006   *Emerging Artist Fellowship Exhibition, 20th Anniversary*, Socrates Sculpture
              Park, Long Island City NY
           Invisible Graffiti: Magnet Show, on-site installation in a Richard Serra
              Torqued Ellipse, Port Morris, Bronx NY

2004   *Albuquerque Contemporary*, Albuquerque Museum, Albuquerque NM

EDUCATION

2002   MFA, Yale University, New Haven CT

1999   New York Studio School of Drawing, Painting & Sculpture,
              New York NY

1999   BA, Dartmouth College, Hanover NH

1998   American University in Perugia, Perugia, Italy

Kade Twist

CHEROKEE
b. 1971, Bakersfield CA
Lives in Tempe AZ
http://www.nativelabs.com

The Way the Sun Rises over Rivers Is No Different Than the Way the Sun Sets over Oceans is a meditation on the contemporary Cherokee diaspora and our search for a sense of place, cultural meaning, and beauty between the Illinois River of Oklahoma and the Pacific Ocean beaches—the idealized geographies that define the Cherokee Nation of Oklahoma and Cherokee diaspora of California.

—Kade Twist

In Kade Twist's *There Is No End of the Trail; There is Merely a System of Prosthesis* (2006–07), a prosthetic leg casts a shadow against the video that plays behind it. Like Kent Monkman, Twist reinterprets James Earle Fraser's infamous *End of the Trail*, though for Twist history is not a farce of seduction and psychological projection, but the experience of phantom pain. Twist was born in Bakersfield, California, far from the Cherokee Nation of Oklahoma, even farther from the original Cherokee territories on the eastern seaboard of the United States. The Cherokee diaspora, which dates to the early 19th century, is the ongoing narrative behind Twist's recent explorations. His new work for this exhibition, *The Way the Sun Rises over Rivers Is No Different Than the Way the Sun Sets over Oceans*, continues the theme of loss and dispersal. Twist's work contains many references that are difficult to untangle without knowledge of the history of the Cherokee people, and of other tribes who suffered similar experiences. What Twist seems to convey, nevertheless, is the critical importance of myth in diasporic conditions if we are to maintain a sense of history, tradition, and identity. The question lingers, Do we want to return home, when return evokes finality and leaving implies a quest? Twist seems to suggest that, whichever we choose, we carry our stories with us to help us negotiate our lives. —GM

please believe me

SELECTED SOLO EXHIBITIONS

2007   *Hunter and Buzzard*, MonOrchid Gallery, Phoenix AZ

SELECTED GROUP EXHIBITIONS

2007   *You Must Return Home (Now!)*, Postcommodity, 4 + 4 Days in
           Motion Festival, Prague, Czech Republic
        All the Way to the Suburbs, Postcommodity, Institute Slavonice, Center
           for the Future, Slavonice, Czech Republic
2006   *Chaos Theory 7*, Legend City, Phoenix AZ
        New American City, Arizona State Museum, Tempe AZ
        The Circumstances in Which Thunder Has Left Us, Paper Heart Gallery,
           Phoenix AZ
2005   *Chaos Theory 6*, Legend City, Phoenix AZ
        Vinyl Moccasins, MonOrchid Gallery, Phoenix AZ
        Suli Is with Us, The Ice House, Phoenix AZ
2004   *Broken Toys*, Buckaroo Parish Gallery, Phoenix AZ
        Language Preservation, Crisis Gallery, Phoenix AZ
        A Storage Shed for My Children, Cone Gallery, Phoenix AZ

SELECTED PERFORMANCES

2006   Poetry reading, Coyote Gallery, Chicago Indian Center, Chicago IL
        Poetry reading, Native American Journalists Association, Tulsa OK
        Performance with noise band Kavigre, Paper Heart Gallery, Phoenix AZ
2005   Performance with Kavigre, The Ice House, Phoenix AZ
2004   Poetry reading, Heard Museum, Phoenix AZ

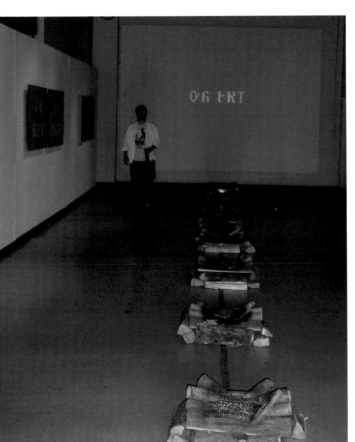

BOOK

Amazing Grace, forthcoming, 2007 First Book Award
           for Poetry from the Native Writers' Circle
           of the Americas

PUBLIC COLLECTION

Arizona State University Art Museum, Tempe AZ

EDUCATION

1999   BA, University of Oklahoma, Norman OK
1999   American Indian Policy Seminar,
           American University, Washington DC

Kade Twist
Prosthetic Faith, 2007
Media installation
MonOrchid Gallery
Courtesy of the artist

Bernard Williams

AFRICAN AMERICAN/NATIVE ANCESTRY
b. 1964, Chicago IL
Lives in Chicago IL and New York NY

My work originates from a "museum aesthetic." I attempt to appropriate some of the formal practice of museums. These institutions around the world hold and collect vast stores of objects, images, and information. Materials are displayed or held carefully out of sight. My recent works display fragments and personal discoveries that are then presented with familiar material. They are highly graphic, congested diagrams that mimic historical collections. They are themselves neither histories, chronologies, nor taxonomies. The interpretations are impulsive and intuitive. They are attempts to manage the overwhelming complexities of constructing histories that evoke worldviews.

—Bernard Williams

When Bernard Williams talks about using a "museum aesthetic" in his work, he may mean that public spaces and institutions create and construct a particular discourse that casts a framework around its subject, and he questions the ethics of this. His *Charting America* (2002–present) begins from a set of signs, black images on a contrasting background, neatly arranged as if they were typeset. As he says, these glyphs are "neither histories, chronologies, nor taxonomies." They can be read in no particular order—indeed, Williams may change their order for an installation. Some of the images are familiar and iconic; some appear made-up. Some are words, others numbers. The icons remind me of Lakota winter counts, or histories, in which the artist/historian set down in a small symbolic image the most important event of each year, creating a chronology of the tribe. As art, Williams's work allows the viewer visual and interpretive authority. Its power lies not just in the images, but in the images' unexpected juxtapositions and resulting, often personal, meanings. Like the best institutions, Williams's museum-on-the-wall invites viewers to come with their sympathies, attitudes, and associations, and to walk away with surprising perceptions. At every turn *Charting America* offers us something we were never told, something we never asked or wanted to know. It reminds us that we are implicated in these narratives: what we were told is too often what we pass on to the next generation. —GM

SELECTED SOLO EXHIBITIONS

2007   *New Sculptures/ The Architect's Table*, Thomas McCormick Gallery,
            Chicago IL
2005   *Wood Words & Lines*, sculpture installation, Indiana University-Gary,
            Gary IN
        Sculpture and wall installation, Chapman University,
            Orange CA
        Legendary Tales, G. R. N'Namdi Gallery, Chicago IL
2004   *Painting and Sculpture*, I SPACE, Chicago IL
        Intersections, Kohler Art Center, Kohler WI
        Fine Arts Work Center, Provincetown MA

SELECTED GROUP EXHIBITIONS

2005   *Two Continents and Beyond: Waterways*, 9th Istanbul Biennale,
            Istanbul, Turkey
        Sculpture on the Grounds, Evanston Art Center, Evanston IL
        The Ornamental Systems of Louis Sullivan, Hyde Park Art Center,
            Chicago IL
        A War-Like People, MonOrchid Gallery, Phoenix AZ
2004   Mural commission, collaboration with students, Indiana
            University-Purdue University, Fort Wayne IN

SELECTED PUBLIC COLLECTIONS

Chicago Transit Authority, Chicago IL
McCormick Place Convention Center, Chicago IL
Eiteljorg Museum, Indianapolis IN
Snite Museum of Art, Notre Dame University, Notre Dame IN
Cook County Hospital, Chicago IL

EDUCATION

1990   MFA, Northwestern
            University, Evanston IL
1988   BFA, University of Illinois,
            Champaign-Urbana IL

Steven Yazzie

NAVAJO/LAGUNA/WELSH
b. 1970
Lives in Phoenix AZ
web.mac.com/stevenyazzie

This work was initially conceived out of a found hubcap and a conversation I had with a friend about the Jeffersonian grid. During the great westward exploration and expansion of the United States, new challenges arose on how to define and divide land. Thomas Jefferson suggested a grid system based on the rectangle. The grid is divided into plots of one mile square, each consisting of 640 acres. The Jeffersonian grid represents a quantitative method for land expansion and is a system we still use to this day in organizing geographic space: Metro-Phoenix and Las Vegas. "Here ye, here ye, just put a rectangle around it." Sleeping with Jefferson is a response to a global experience more frequently predetermined by algorithms and computer models and is about the long-drawn-out philosophical bloodlines we have created and destroyed, through progress, necessity, choice, and best-case scenarios.

—Steven Yazzie

Steven Yazzie uses humor and other literary tropes that push at the incongruities of life. In *Sleeping with Jefferson*, his rhetorical device is irony. We ask manufacturers to engineer cars that are less dependent on fossil fuels, whose effects on the global environment are argued to be devastating. Yet, designers and manufacturers continue to build and sell oversized vehicles to those able to afford them—some would say, to those with egos large enough to ignore the environment. By polishing hubcaps, squaring them off, and arranging them in a grid, Yazzie has changed their dynamic, like Native Americans of the past who saw the aesthetics in gun flintlocks and turned them into art. Looking at Yazzie's sculpture, do we think of vehicles? Not really. His hubcaps signify a transformation of our time, a reformulation of and new way to consider the ideology of planned obsolescence. —GM

SOLO EXHIBITION

2005   *Steven Yazzie—New Work*, Blue Gallery, Kansas City MO

SELECTED GROUP EXHIBITIONS

2007   4 + 4 Days in Motion Festival, Postcommodity, Prague, Czech Republic
          Intersections, Postcommodity, Slavonice, Czech Republic
          Hi ha alguna cosa de revolucionarien tot aco, Sala Parpallo, Valencia, Spain
          Drawing Outside the Lines, Scottsdale Museum of Contemporary Art,
             Scottsdale AZ
          New Works, Berlin Gallery, Phoenix AZ
          Draw Me a Picture, Heard Museum, Phoenix AZ
2006   *Saints and Sirens*, Blue Gallery, Kansas City MO
          DECK – Skatedeck Art Exhibit, Ice House, Phoenix AZ
2005   *Identity: Divided Transformations*, Phoenix College, Phoenix AZ
          Exhibition at Credit Suisse First Boston, New York NY
          Contemporary Forum Grant Winners, Phoenix Art Museum,
             Phoenix AZ
2004–07 *Kaos Theory*, Legend City Studios, Phoenix AZ
2003–07 Contemporary Forum Auction, Phoenix Art Museum, Phoenix AZ

PUBLIC COLLECTIONS

Mayo Clinic, Phoenix and Scottsdale AZ
Heard Museum, Phoenix AZ

EDUCATION

Phoenix College, Phoenix AZ
United States Marine Corps

front.

back.

WOUNDED KNEE SKATEBOARD MANUFACTURING & PROPAGANDA

JOHN HAWORTH

Intersections: Broadway and Central

Last June, I poked my head into the conference room at the National Museum of the American Indian's Heye Center to ask a colleague a quick question. Seated at the table was a creative group having an energetic conversation about contemporary Native art and life. The young man at the center of the discussion reached in his tote bag and brought out a T-shirt manufactured by his company, Wounded Knee Skateboards, printed with the words "No Surrender—Tashunca-Utitco" over a symbol for the four directions. On the back of the shirt was a vivid image of the warrior Crazy Horse. His horse stood on black earth against a vibrant yellow and red sky—Lakota colors. Bold block capitals read, "IT IS A GOOD DAY TO DIE," underscored by even larger, bolder type saying, "WOUNDED KNEE." The tag line was, "SKATEBOARD MANUFACTURING & PROPOGANDA." Our guest was Jim Murphy (Lenni Lenape), and he was talking about how important skateboarding is to many young Native Americans. Who knew?

How appropriate, then, that *Remix* includes a video installation piece about Native American skateboarders. Dustinn Craig, an artist of White Mountain Apache and Navajo heritage, entitles his piece *4-Wheel Warpony*, and he shows us that, for some Indian young people, skateboarding is a way to celebrate and honor their Native identity and sense of community.

We appreciate art for its intrinsic qualities of aesthetic vision, technical mastery, and individual emotion and insight, but we also understand art's role as social commentary and critique—as both wake-up call and invitation to check out what's new. *Remix* recognizes that contemporary Native artists have much to tell us about our world that is grounded in their unique perspectives and cultural backgrounds. These artists all have deeply held opinions, worldviews formed at the intersection of traditional and postmodern expression, and an urgency to find media and language to express complex ideas. Their work speaks about geographic, generational, cultural, and psychological boundaries. They address both social possibilities and limitations, often referencing movement and motion: hitchhiking, dancing, spiritual and political transformation, and, yes, skateboard-

John Pearson
T-shirt and deck designs for
Wounded Knee Skateboards
Courtesy of Jim Murphy,
Wounded Knee Skateboards

Dustinn Craig
4-Wheel Warpony, 2007
Video
Courtesy of the artist

ing. These artists explore the mix of high and low, popular and fine, historic and contemporary, communal and universal. Some incorporate irony and humor in their art to make provocative and clever points. All remind us to pay closer attention to the complicated history and 21st-century culture not only of the United States, but also of Canada and Mexico.

Arts writer Dave Hickey refers to contemporary art discourse as being about money, sex, and blood—class, gender, and identity.[1] Economic survival and social dislocation are no less front-burner issues for Native America, and therefore Native artists. The assertion of identity—"Nativeness"—has been a recurring theme in Native art production for decades, as have maintaining and sustaining culture, family, and community. Native art has long asked how people might balance traditional life and the modern world, or navigate being Native in a non-Native society. The stunning and powerful pieces in *Remix* explode old dichotomies into multiple pieces. These works are about globalization, or what it means to be of mixed heritage with (or sometimes without) strong connections to one or more Native communities. Migration and urban life are also striking counterpoints to how Native artists from earlier times experienced a different world.

When I lived in Phoenix in the early 1970s, Arizona actively promoted its Indian heritage to the "snowbirds" and local citizens. Think *Arizona Highways*. Think Sun City. The state's leading cultural institution presenting Native arts and cultures, then as now, was the Heard Museum, on Central Avenue, and its focus was historical and traditional. When I moved to New York City in the middle of that decade, I found myself in another hot place—not thanks to the climate (although August in New York is sweltering), but because the downtown art scene was one of the most exciting creative communities in the world. Far uptown, the Museum of the American Indian, whose collections later became the cornerstone of the Smithsonian's National Museum of the American Indian, was the only cultural institution in New York City dedicated exclusively to American Indian culture, and its focus, too, was historical.

Jump cut, as Joe Baker might say, to today. The Heard and the National Museum of the American Indian continue to draw upon important, historically significant collections and to have deep respect for the Native material culture and traditions represented in the objects entrusted to our care. Yet for both the Heard, in what is now the fifth largest city in the United States, and NMAI's Heye Center, in lower Manhattan, the presentation of contemporary Native art has come to occupy a much more prominent place in our respective programs. Changes in the broader cultural landscape that informs our work have led us to make this shift, which invigorates our work and opens our institutions to exciting new possibilities.

NEW MODERNITIES IN A POST-INDIAN WORLD

Photo Credits

All artwork and photography © the artist unless otherwise noted.

Cover, Steven Yazzie

pp. 2–3, photo montage by Kate Johnson, images provided by the artists

p. 6, photo montage by Steve Bell, images provided by the artists

p. 9, Dustinn Craig

p. 10, photo montage by Steve Bell, images provided by the artists

p. 14, James Prinz

pp. 16–17, Steve Clique

p. 19, James Prinz

pp. 20-21, © Nadia Myre/ licensed by SODART, Montréal, and VAGA, New York

p. 23, Kent Monkman

p. 24, Brian Miller

p. 25, Anna Tsouhlarakis

p. 27, Frederieke Taylor Gallery

p. 29, Bentley Gallery

p. 30, Lee Lusby / 337 Photo

p. 33, sunset/sunrise, Nathan H. Young; text, Kade Twist

p. 34, Steven Yazzie

p. 36, Brandon Sullivan

p. 39, Bentley Gallery

pp. 40, 41, Lee Lusby/337 Photo

p. 42, David Alfya

p. 43, Isaac Applebaum

p. 44, Alan Natachu

p. 45, upper, Anna Tsouhlarakis

p. 45, lower, Frederieke Taylor Gallery

p. 46, upper, photo by Denis Farley; lower, Art Mûr. © Nadia Myre/licensed by SODART, Montréal, and VAGA, New York

p. 47, Tom Van Eynde

p. 48, David Hannan

pp. 49–51, Dustinn Craig

p. 52, Craig Smith

p. 54, David Alfya

p. 57, Craig Smith

pp. 58–59, Brian Miller

pp. 60–61, Dustinn Craig

pp. 62-63, Fausto Fernandez; collage, Craig Smith

pp. 64-65, Luis Gutierrez

pp. 66-67, David Hannan

pp. 68–69, Gregory Lomayesva

pp. 70–71, Brian Miller

pp. 72–73, Franco Mondini-Ruiz

p. 74, Kent Monkman

p. 75, Kent Monkman and Chris Chapman

pp. 76–77, Nadia Myre

pp. 78–79, Alan Natachu

pp. 80-81, Hector Ruiz

pp. 82–83, Anna Tsouhlarakis

pp. 84–85, Kade Twist

pp. 86–87, Bernard Williams

pp. 88-89, Steven Yazzie

p. 90, courtesy of Jim Murphy

p. 93, Dustinn Craig

Endnotes

All artists' quotations, unless otherwise noted, were provided by the artists for this project.

Interventions: Making a New Space for Indigenous Art

Opening quotation: Alan Gilbert, *Another Future: Poetry and Art in a Postmodern Twilight*. Wesleyan University Press, 2006.

1. Olu Oguibe, *Double Dutch and the Culture Game*, University of Minnesota Press, 2004, p. 33.

2. Men in Black, *Handbook of Curatorial Practice*, Christoph Tannert/Ute Tischler, eds. Berlin: Kunstlerhaus Bethanien,2003, p. 89.

3. Quoted in Olu Oguibe, *Represent'n: The Young Generation in African American Art*, University of Minnesota Press, 2004, p. 122.

4. Kathryn Kramer, *Beyond Stereotype: Works by Kori Newkirk and Bernard Williams,* Dowd Fine Arts Gallery, State University of New York College at Cortland, 2002, p. 8.

5. James Martin, "Nadia Myre's Art Project Is Already at the McCord," *Concordia's Thursday Report Online*, June 6, 2002. ctr.concordia.ca/2001-02/june6/08-Myre/index.shtml.

6. Robert Houle, excerpt from a gallery publication, Paul Petro Contemporary Art, 2004.

7. Liz Kotz, "Video Projection, the Space between Screens," in *Theory in Contemporary Art since 1985*, Zoya Kocur and Simon Leung, eds. Blackwell Publishing, 2005, p. 102.

8. Kent Monkman, artist statement, 2006.

9. Brian Miller, artist statement and project summary, 2004.

10. Paulo Herkenhoff, in *Ultra Baroque: Aspects of Post Latin American Art*, Elizabeth Armstrong & Victor Zamudio-Taylor, eds. Museum of Contemporary Art, San Diego, 2000, p. 134.

11. Elizabeth Armstrong & Victor Zamudio-Taylor, *Ultra Baroque: Aspects of Post Latin American Art*, Museum of Contemporary Art, San Diego, 2000, p. 70.

12. Lara Taubman, *The Truth of the Region: Recent Works by Hector Ruiz*, Heard Museum, 2006, p. 1.

13. Kade L. Twist, "Hunter & Buzzard: Suburban NDN Meta-narratives," blog entry dated Feb. 21, 2007. http://kadeltwist.blogspot.com.

14. Marilu Knode, exhibition prospectus for *Speed Trap*, 2007.

15. Christopher Maurer, *Fortune's Favorite Child: The Uneasy Life of Walter Anderson*, University Press of Mississippi/Jackson, 2003, p. 290.

Autobiographical texts throughout are from an unpublished manuscript by Joe Baker.

Native Identity in an Age of Hybridity

1. Lucy Lippard, *The Lure of the Local: Senses of Place in a Multi-centered Society,* The New Press, 1997, p. 71.

2. James Clifford, *The Predicament of Culture: Twentieth Century Ethnography, Literature, and Art*, Harvard University Press, 1988, p. 289.

3. Email to the author, April 2007.

Introductions: Mixing It Up

1. Joe Baker and Lara Taubman, *Diaspora*, Heard Museum, Phoenix AZ, April 8-December 31, 2006.

2. Fausto Fernandez, artist's page, the Latin American Art Gallery. http://www.thelatinamericanartgallery.com/artist/artist.php?artistId=1009.

3. Matthew Bowman, interview with Luis Daniel Guiterrez, *Phoenix Art Space*, April 8, 2007. http://www.phoenixartspace.com/viewarticle.php?ID=124.

4. Lomayesva statement: Jackson, Devon, "Artist with an Attitude," *Southwest Art*, January 2004, p.80.

5. Franco Mondini-Ruiz, interviewed by Jeffrey Brown, "New Mexico Celebrates Hispanic Culture," *PBS Newshour*, May 30, 2007. http://www.pbs.org/newshour/bb/entertainment/jan-june07/alameda_05-30.html.

6. Nadia Myre, Studio/Bio, Terminus 1525.ca. http://www.terminus1525.ca/studio/about/5491.

7. Yasmin Khan, "Native Art," *Santa Fe New Mexican*, July 24, 2004. www.santafenewmexican.com/news/2261.html.

8. Brenda Norrell, "Border Revelations, Aleut Jewels and Kickapoo Folk Art," *Indian Country Today*, March 7, 2006, p. 1. http://www.indiancountry.com/content.cfm?id=1096412592.

Intersections: Broadway and Central

1. Dave Hickey, *Air Guitar*, Art Issues Press, 1997.

Authors

JOE BAKER (Delaware), artist, educator, and Lloyd Kiva New Curator of Contemporary Art at the Heard, has pioneered opportunities for emerging and under-represented artists through a series of one-person exhibitions, *Artspeak: New Voices in Contemporary Expression*. He is the recipient of the Virginia Piper Charitable Trust 2005 Fellows Award, recognizing outstanding leaders in nonprofit communities, and the Scottsdale Museum of Contemporary Art's Contemporary Catalyst Award for 2007. In 2003, he was honored by his peers with a Joan Mitchell Foundation Award for painting. Baker's diverse career in the arts includes performances with the Phoenix Dance Company and off Broadway at the Cubiculo Theatre, New York.

ELEANOR HEARTNEY is an award-winning critic and contributing editor to *Art in America* and *Artpress*. She is the author of *Critical Condition: American Culture at the Crossroads* (1997), *Postmodernism* (2001), *Postmodern Heretics: The Catholic Imagination in Contemporary Art* (2004), and *Defending Complexity: Art, Politics and the New World Order* (2006), and co-author of *After the Revolution: Women Who Transformed Contemporary Art* (2007). *Art and Today*, her survey of the contemporary art of the last 25 years, will be published in spring 2008.

GERALD McMASTER (Plains Cree and member of the Siksika Nation), an artist and curator of Canadian art at the Art Gallery of Ontario in Toronto, has been honored with the National Aboriginal Achievement Award, the ICOM-Canada Prize for contributions to museology, and the Order of Canada, that nation's highest recognition. As assistant director for cultural resources at NMAI, McMaster joined Clifford E. Trafzer in editing *Native Universe: Voices from Indian America* (2004), the museum's landmark book. McMaster, who grew up on the Red Pheasant Reserve in Saskatchewan, holds a PhD from the University of Amsterdam and degrees from the Institute of American Indian Arts, the Minneapolis College of Art and Design, and Carleton University.

JOHN HAWORTH (Cherokee), director of NMAI's George Gustav Heye Center, began his career with the National Endowment for the Arts, developing arts programming in his home state of Oklahoma, and in a similar position with the Arizona Arts and Humanities Commission. Haworth moved to New York in the mid 1970s to work with grassroots arts organizations. Before joining NMAI in 1995, he served as Assistant Commissioner for Cultural Institutions at the New York City Department of Cultural Affairs. His essays have appeared in numerous publications, including, most recently, *Off the Map: Landscape in the Native Imagination* (2007).